The
DAILY BIBLE®

30 Days
through Psalms
and Proverbs

F. LaGard Smith

HARVEST HOUSE PUBLISHERS
EUGENE, OREGON

Cover by Koechel Peterson & Associates, Inc., Minneapolis, Minnesota

30 DAYS THROUGH PSALMS AND PROVERBS
Copyright © 2004 by F. LaGard Smith
Published by Harvest House Publishers
Eugene, Oregon 97402
www.harvesthousepublishers.com

Smith, F. LaGard (Frank LaGard), 1944-
  30 days through Psalms and Proverbs / F. LaGard Smith.
     p. cm.
  ISBN 0-7369-0866-8 (pbk.)
  1. Bible. O.T. Psalms—Meditations. 2. Bible. O.T. Proverbs—Meditations. 3. Devotional calendars. I. Title: Thirty days through Psalms and Proverbs. II. Title: At head of title: Daily Bible. III. Title.
  BS1430.55.S65 2004
  223'.206—dc22   2003015759

Printed in the United States of America

    04 05 06 07 08 09 10 11 /BP-KB/ 10 9 8 7 6

Contents

Introduction

ARE YOU HAPPY? IF YOUR ANSWER IS NO, have you thought about why? Are you in a difficult relationship, or are things not going well at work? Is someone you love hurting himself through drug or alcohol dependence? Are you worried about where the next rent check or mortgage payment will come from?

If nothing catastrophic is happening in your life, are you nevertheless aimless or bored? Do you wonder what life is all about? Do you think about how you could be more fulfilled or lead a more enriching life?

Maybe you have tried to change your circumstances but have run into difficult barriers. Perhaps your life is in good shape except for some area that you would like to do something about but can't seem to get under control. Where should you look for answers? Who can help you solve your problems?

Would you be surprised to learn that our problems are not very different from those that people who lived centuries ago encountered? Human beings have not changed much over the years. Nor have their problems. In fact, some ancient writings about the meaning of life and how to live it sound as if they were written yesterday. They are found in the book of Proverbs.

Most of Proverbs is made up of short poems, usually in the form of couplets, which present comparative or antithetical imagery. The wise king Solomon wrote literally thousands of proverbs. More than 500 of these are collected in the book of Proverbs. The wise sayings of Israel's elders are also included.

The purpose of Proverbs is to promote ethical standards and to give practical advice for everyday living. Proverbs places high value on the need for insight, and it also provides that insight. Yet the proverbs of Israel are unique: Their wisdom does not come from human experience. The writers of Proverbs point the reader to the God of creation. He knows how we function best. God has revealed His divine insight to us so that we may live up to our potential.

Reading Proverbs is no academic exercise. It is a life-changing experience. In Proverbs we find not only solutions to our problems but also advice that will keep us out of trouble to begin with. We learn about who we are and what makes us happy. We learn about proper relationships with God and our fellow humans. We are told what things are most important in life and how we can attain them.

What we learn from Proverbs is that nothing is more important than loving God and following His divine guidance. Rules are hard to keep, and practical advice is hard to follow. Therefore God has given us more than intellectual understanding. He has called us into a relationship with Himself so that we can have not only an abundant life in this world but also eternal life after death.

The ageless wisdom of Proverbs is presented here in 30 sections, providing an enriching month of spiritual insight for those who desire to read on a daily basis.

Coming as no surprise, the wisdom found in Proverbs dovetails perfectly with corresponding sentiments contained in Psalms. These two collections of literature have not only the same divine source but also principle writers who were father and son. What the wise king Solomon passed along from his head by way of practical proverbs, his father, King David, had already experienced in his heart.

Coupled with the common hand of inspiration is the intriguing possibility that David's heart-wrenching and agonizing struggles had produced a wisdom from above that he passed along to his son. Whereas Solomon had asked God for the gift of wisdom, David had gained wisdom and insight the hard way—often through his own grievous sin.

A reader of Psalms also gets a sense that David had frequently been on the receiving end of the folly that comes when wisdom goes unheeded. If Solomon writes with hopeful aspiration about the blessing of following God's wisdom, David seems to be haunted by wicked fools intent on doing him harm. Little wonder that we sometimes see David calling on God to be vindictive to enemies who themselves were being vindictive! David is so intent on righting the wrongs of those who have acted foolishly that he appears to contradict the very wisdom he is trying to uphold.

When heart and mind intersect with such keen insight and heartfelt passion, we are brought before the throne of God, who is both infinitely wise and infinitely caring—not just for David and Solomon but also for you and me. No wonder Psalms is filled with praises to God our Maker, Redeemer, and Defender. Praise God for both mind and heart! For wisdom and passion! For insights too wonderful for man to have discovered on his own, and for men whose hearts were as vulnerable as ours, whose shared pain we know all too well.

May God bless this presentation of Scripture to all who seek to live happy and abundant lives through reading His holy Word.

— F. LaGard Smith

Life-Changing Insight

Do you remember your favorite teachers? Isn't what you appreciated most about them the fact that they challenged your thinking, stretched your perspective, and introduced you to wonderful new ideas? That is one reason we love our parents: They were the most influential teachers of all. We learned more than mere information from our parents and teachers; we learned insight and understanding. More than anything else, they gave guidance and direction to lead us through our early years.

As we grow older, we face a more complicated world. How are we to cope with broken relationships, financial stress, compulsive habits, guilty feelings, struggles with temptation, or self-doubt? How are we to live each day with newspaper headlines reminding us of all that is wrong with our world, or worse yet, with friends or loved ones reminding us of all that is wrong with us?

Where do we turn to get a better focus on life? Who has the agenda to get us through each hectic day? In a world of distortion, who has the true picture? When so much is wrong, who knows what is right?

In a time not greatly different from our own, Solomon had a favorite teacher who taught him about life and about living. She knew what was real and what was deceptive, what was right and what was wrong. She told him how to live a full and happy life. She always had good judgment. Kings sought her advice. They considered her counsel more valuable than all the wealth of their nations. Who is this teacher? Her name is Wisdom.

How could Wisdom have such insight? Solomon tells us that Wisdom was with God in the beginning, before the world existed. God's Wisdom was involved in the creation of the universe and, therefore, knows our world inside and out. Wisdom knows us better than we know ourselves. Wisdom understands our needs and desires. Wisdom understands how we can have power over our lives and how we hurt ourselves when we fail to follow her advice.

Wisdom also knows that we tend to ignore her. So, as a teacher with treasures to share, she calls out to each one of us.

Proverbs

Wisdom as Teacher

Does not wisdom call out?
    Does not understanding raise her voice?
On the heights along the way,
    where the paths meet, she takes her stand;
beside the gates leading into the city,
    at the entrances, she cries aloud:
"To you, O men, I call out;
    I raise my voice to all mankind.
You who are simple, gain prudence;
    you who are foolish, gain understanding.
Listen, for I have worthy things to say;
    I open my lips to speak what is right.
My mouth speaks what is true,
    for my lips detest wickedness.

All the words of my mouth are just;
    none of them is crooked or perverse.
To the discerning all of them are right;
    they are faultless to those who have
        knowledge.
Choose my instruction instead of silver,
    knowledge rather than choice gold,
for wisdom is more precious than rubies,
    and nothing you desire can compare with her.

"I, wisdom, dwell together with prudence;
    I possess knowledge and discretion.
To fear the LORD is to hate evil;
    I hate pride and arrogance,
    evil behavior and perverse speech.
Counsel and sound judgment are mine;
    I have understanding and power.
By me kings reign
    and rulers make laws that are just;
by me princes govern,
    and all nobles who rule on earth.
I love those who love me,
    and those who seek me find me.
With me are riches and honor,
    enduring wealth and prosperity.
My fruit is better than fine gold;
    what I yield surpasses choice silver.
I walk in the way of righteousness,
    along the paths of justice,
bestowing wealth on those who love me
    and making their treasuries full.

"The LORD brought me forth as the first of his
        works,
    before his deeds of old;

I was appointed from eternity,
    from the beginning, before the world began.
When there were no oceans, I was given birth,
    when there were no springs abounding
            with water;
before the mountains were settled in place,
    before the hills, I was given birth,
before he made the earth or its fields
    or any of the dust of the world.
I was there when he set the heavens in place,
    when he marked out the horizon on the
            face of the deep,
when he established the clouds above
    and fixed securely the fountains of the deep,
when he gave the sea its boundary
    so the waters would not overstep his
            command,
and when he marked out the foundations
            of the earth.
    Then I was the craftsman at his side.
I was filled with delight day after day,
    rejoicing always in his presence,
rejoicing in his whole world
    and delighting in mankind.

"Now then, my sons, listen to me;
    blessed are those who keep my ways.
Listen to my instruction and be wise;
    do not ignore it.
Blessed is the man who listens to me,
    watching daily at my doors,
    waiting at my doorway.
For whoever finds me finds life
    and receives favor from the LORD.
But whoever fails to find me harms himself;
    all who hate me love death."

PROVERBS 8

Wisdom has built her house;
>she has hewn out its seven pillars.
She has prepared her meat and mixed her wine;
>she has also set her table.
She has sent out her maids, and she calls
>from the highest point of the city.
"Let all who are simple come in here!"
>she says to those who lack judgment.
"Come, eat my food
>and drink the wine I have mixed.
Leave your simple ways and you will live;
>walk in the way of understanding.

PROVERBS 9:1-6

Psalms

SOLOMON'S TEACHER, WISDOM, CALLS OUT TO each of us to come near and learn the lessons of a happy and secure life. Where is Wisdom to be found? David points us to God's own Word—in the form of divinely revealed statutes, precepts, commands, and ordinances.

Are we so awed by God's grace that law seems an altogether unlikely source of divine wisdom? Perhaps we'd be wise to think again. Without discounting God's grace in the least, God's eternal law—in unyielding black and white—is still the quintessential source of life, light, and—in the end—pure joy.

The heavens declare the glory of God;
>the skies proclaim the work of his hands.
Day after day they pour forth speech;
>night after night they display knowledge.
There is no speech or language
>where their voice is not heard.

Their voice goes out into all the earth,
their words to the ends of the world.

In the heavens he has pitched a tent for the sun,
which is like a bridegroom coming forth
from his pavilion,
like a champion rejoicing to run his course.
It rises at one end of the heavens
and makes its circuit to the other;
nothing is hidden from its heat.

The law of the Lord is perfect,
reviving the soul.
The statutes of the Lord are trustworthy,
making wise the simple.
The precepts of the Lord are right,
giving joy to the heart.
The commands of the Lord are radiant,
giving light to the eyes.
The fear of the Lord is pure,
enduring forever.
The ordinances of the Lord are sure
and altogether righteous.
They are more precious than gold,
than much pure gold;
they are sweeter than honey,
than honey from the comb.
By them is your servant warned;
in keeping them there is great reward.

Who can discern his errors?
Forgive my hidden faults.
Keep your servant also from willful sins;
may they not rule over me.

LIFE-CHANGING INSIGHT

Then will I be blameless,
    innocent of great transgression.

May the words of my mouth and the meditation
        of my heart
    be pleasing in your sight,
    O LORD, my Rock and my Redeemer.

PSALM 19

On God's Inside Track

WHAT DO YOU VALUE MOST? YOUR POSSESSIONS? Your health? Your family? Suppose you lost them all. What would life mean to you then? Could you accept life as it comes? Only a strong person with strong character can keep living with hope under such circumstances. Yet we do not have to experience total loss to feel the need for strength greater than our own. Can Wisdom help us?

Wisdom can be our guide, but Wisdom does not speak from her own storehouse of knowledge. She is not abstract reason, accumulated experience, or self-knowledge. Wisdom leads us not to herself but to a personal God who cares.

Our search for understanding must take us to God, who created us. If we are willing to accept His lordship in our lives, we will come to a true knowledge of God. That knowledge will bring us the direction and power we need to confront the challenges of each new day.

By leading us to a knowledge of God and His will for our lives, Wisdom protects us from people and circum-stances that would destroy us. Wisdom can keep us from losing, through our own fault, the most important things: our spiritual vitality, the love in our families, our sense of fulfillment and purpose, and perhaps even our health.

When we know God personally, Wisdom can bring us a richness of life, safe from pitfalls and free from fear.

Proverbs

The Value of Wisdom

My son, if you accept my words
    and store up my commands within you,
turning your ear to wisdom
    and applying your heart to understanding,
and if you call out for insight
    and cry aloud for understanding,
and if you look for it as for silver
    and search for it as for hidden treasure
then you will understand the fear of the LORD
    and find the knowledge of God.
For the LORD gives wisdom,
    and from his mouth come knowledge and
        understanding.
He holds victory in store for the upright,
    he is a shield to those whose walk is blameless,
for he guards the course of the just
    and protects the way of his faithful ones.

Then you will understand what is right and just
    and fair—every good path.
For wisdom will enter your heart,
    and knowledge will be pleasant to your soul.
Discretion will protect you,
    and understanding will guard you.

Wisdom will save you from the ways of wicked men,
    from men whose words are perverse,

who leave the straight paths
    to walk in dark ways,
who delight in doing wrong
    and rejoice in the perverseness of evil,
whose paths are crooked
    and who are devious in their ways.

It will save you also from the adulteress,
    from the wayward wife with her seductive words,
who has left the partner of her youth
    and ignored the covenant she made before God.
For her house leads down to death
    and her paths to the spirits of the dead.
None who go to her return
    or attain the paths of life.

Thus you will walk in the ways of good men
    and keep to the paths of the righteous.
For the upright will live in the land,
    and the blameless will remain in it:
but the wicked will be cut off from the land,
    and the unfaithful will be torn from it.

PROVERBS 2

Blessed is the man who finds wisdom,
    the man who gains understanding,
for she is more profitable than silver
    and yields better returns than gold.
She is more precious than rubies;
    nothing you desire can compare with her.
Long life is in her right hand;
    in her left hand are riches and honor.
Her ways are pleasant ways,
    and all her paths are peace.

She is a tree of life to those who embrace her;
  those who lay hold of her will be blessed.

By wisdom the LORD laid the earth's foundations,
  by understanding he set the heavens in place;
by his knowledge the deeps were divided,
  and the clouds let drop the dew.

My son, preserve sound judgment and discernment,
  do not let them out of your sight;
they will be life for you,
  an ornament to grace your neck.
Then you will go on your way in safety,
  and your foot will not stumble;
when you lie down, you will not be afraid;
  when you lie down, your sleep will be sweet.

PROVERBS 3:13-24

Psalms

AH, TO SLEEP SOUNDLY, KNOWING THAT EVERY ASPECT of our lives is better because we honor God's law in all that we do—or would be better if we followed His law more closely. Some people count sheep to fall asleep. The psalmist had a better way to avoid insomnia at the end of the day. All day long he meditated on the precepts and promises in God's law.

What do you think about all day? Do you regularly take time to delve into the Word? If so, do you find yourself reflecting on what it means for your life, or are you like those of us who have so compartmentalized our busy lives that we easily forget in the afternoon what we've read in the morning? You have no guarantee, of course, but you just might sleep better tonight simply because you are spending time right now reflecting on wisdom from above.

> Oh, how I love your law!
>> I meditate on it all day long.
> Your commands make me wiser than my enemies,
>> for they are ever with me.
> I have more insight than all my teachers,
>> for I meditate on your statutes.
> I have more understanding than the elders,
>> for I obey your precepts.
> I have kept my feet from every evil path
>> so that I might obey your word.
> I have not departed from your laws,
>> for you yourself have taught me.
> How sweet are your words to my taste,
>> sweeter than honey to my mouth!
> I gain understanding from your precepts;
>> therefore I hate every wrong path.
>
> Your word is a lamp to my feet
>> and a light for my path.
> I have taken an oath and confirmed it,
>> that I will follow your righteous laws.
> I have suffered much;
>> preserve my life, O LORD, according to your word.
> Accept, O LORD, the willing praise of my mouth,
>> and teach me your laws.
> Though I constantly take my life in my hands,
>> I will not forget your law.
> The wicked have set a snare for me,
>> but I have not strayed from your precepts.
> Your statutes are my heritage forever;
>> they are the joy of my heart.
> My heart is set on keeping your decrees
>> to the very end.

PSALM 119:97-112

Living Without Regret

How many times have you regretted doing or failing to do something? Usually we act upon impulse, without careful thought or consideration. Even more frustrating is our tendency to ignore good advice, only to experience disastrous results. Sometimes we simply fail to ask for advice when we easily could.

How well Wisdom knows us! Wisdom knows our pride and our stubbornness. Wisdom knows that we foolishly trust our own understanding for solutions to our problems. Wisdom knows how often we fail.

But can Wisdom help when we refuse to listen? After the inevitable consequences of our conduct occur, we have missed an opportunity to benefit from Wisdom's warnings. Rarely can we undo the damage we have done. And reliving a foolish life is impossible. Why then do we ignore Wisdom?

Competing with Wisdom for our attention is Folly. Folly is seductive. Folly promises us all we ever wanted—pleasure, excitement, a life of ease. We never seem to learn that Folly is a fraud. Instead of enjoying the excitement we are promised, we are left unfulfilled. Instead of pleasure, we have pain. Instead of ease, we live with anxiety.

Wisdom delivers on her promises. Wisdom demands discipline but rewards us with freedom. Wisdom insists on integrity but gives us peace of mind. When one follows Wisdom, the gratification may be deferred—but how sweet the satisfaction when it comes!

Folly asks the least of us, so we would rather listen to her. But, as Wisdom knows, Folly leads us to emptiness, sadness, and lasting regret.

Proverbs

Fools and Folly

Wisdom calls aloud in the street,
>   she raises her voice in the public squares;
at the head of the noisy streets she cries out,
>   in the gateways of the city she makes her speech:

"How long will you simple ones love your
>   simple ways?
>   How long will mockers delight in mockery
>   and fools hate knowledge?
If you had responded to my rebuke,
>   I would have poured out my heart to you
>   and made my thoughts known to you.
But since you rejected me when I called
>   and no one gave heed when I stretched out
>   my hand,
since you ignored all my advice
>   and would not accept my rebuke,
I in turn will laugh at your disaster;
>   I will mock when calamity overtakes you—
when calamity overtakes you like a storm,
>   when disaster sweeps over you like a whirlwind,
>   when distress and trouble overwhelm you.

"Then they will call to me but I will not answer;
　　they will look for me but will not find me.
Since they hated knowledge
　　and did not choose to fear the LORD,
since they would not accept my advice
　　and spurned my rebuke,
they will eat the fruit of their ways
　　and be filled with the fruit of their schemes.
For the waywardness of the simple will kill them,
　　and the complacency of fools will destroy them;
but whoever listens to me will live in safety
　　and be at ease, without fear of harm."

PROVERBS 1:20-33

The woman Folly is loud;
　　she is undisciplined and without knowledge.
She sits at the door of her house,
　　on a seat at the highest point of the city,
calling out to those who pass by,
　　who go straight on their way.
"Let all who are simple come in here!"
　　she says to those who lack judgment.
"Stolen water is sweet;
　　food eaten in secret is delicious!"
But little do they know that the dead are there,
　　that her guests are in the depths of the grave.

PROVERBS 9:13-18

Psalms

THE ULTIMATE FOLLY IS NOT SIMPLY REJECTING the call of
Wisdom but denying the existence of a God from whom
Wisdom emanates. Anyone who can look at the orderli-
ness, beauty, and power of the universe and still refuse to

believe in a Divine Intelligence behind it all is a fool of the highest order. He who believes that man has created the very idea of God in his own mind—as if wishful thinking—has abandoned his mind and betrayed appalling ignorance.

Such persons need not be serial killers or child rapists. Let a society live according to agnostic and atheistic delusions and one invariably will observe foolish conduct as well as foolish unbelief.

> The fool says in his heart,
>> "There is no God."
> They are corrupt, their deeds are vile;
>> there is no one who does good.

> The Lord looks down from heaven
>> on the sons of men
> to see if there are any who understand,
>> any who seek God.
> All have turned aside,
>> they have together become corrupt;
> there is no one who does good,
>> not even one.

> Will evildoers never learn—
>> those who devour my people as men eat bread
>> and who do not call on the Lord?
> There they are, overwhelmed with dread,
>> for God is present in the company of the righteous.
> You evildoers frustrate the plans of the poor,
>> but the Lord is their refuge.

> Oh, that salvation for Israel would come out of Zion!
>> When the Lord restores the fortunes of his people,
>> let Jacob rejoice and Israel be glad!

Psalm 14

A Father's Precious Gift

WHAT IS THE MOST IMPORTANT LEGACY A PARENT can give to a child? Surely not money or a family name. A wealthy estate may be a curse and the family tree an embarrassment. The wise King Solomon knew what would be best to give to his children—something more valuable than his gold or vast lands. Solomon's greatest legacy was itself a hand-me-down from his father, King David. It was simply good fatherly advice.

The advice? At all cost, find life's meaning by knowing the God who made you. Get to know Wisdom, and follow her teachings. Once you understand your purpose for living, then put it into your heart, make it your top priority, and always act according to it.

Solomon saw the value of this advice in his own life. When given the choice of wealth, power, or fame, he chose Wisdom. For his decision he received not only Wisdom but also wealth, power, and fame. Only in later years, when he neglected his own advice, did he think of life as empty and meaningless.

Sadly, Solomon's sons refused their father's richest legacy. They foolishly confused desired ends with necessary means. They wanted results without effort, institutions without foundation, externals without internals, meaning without understanding. In the end they lost the wealth, power, and fame that otherwise would have been a legacy from their father.

We do not have to repeat their mistake. As Solomon's spiritual children, we can make better decisions and share in his royal legacy. The choice is ours.

Proverbs

Advice and Instruction

Listen, my sons, to a father's instruction;
 pay attention and gain understanding.
I give you sound learning,
 so do not forsake my teaching.
When I was a boy in my father's house,
 still tender, and an only child of my mother,
he taught me and said,
 "Lay hold of my words with all your heart;
 keep my commands and you will live.
Get wisdom, get understanding;
 do not forget my words or swerve from them.
Do not forsake wisdom, and she will protect you;
 love her, and she will watch over you.
Wisdom is supreme; therefore get wisdom.
 Though it cost all you have, get understanding.
Esteem her, and she will exalt you;
 embrace her, and she will honor you.
She will set a garland of grace on your head
 and present you with a crown of splendor."

Listen, my son, accept what I say,
 and the years for your life will be many.
I guide you in the way of wisdom
 and lead you along straight paths.

When you walk, your steps will not be hampered;
    when you run, you will not stumble.
Hold on to instruction, do not let it go;
    guard it well, for it is your life.
Do not set foot on the path of the wicked
    or walk in the way of the evil men.
Avoid it, do not travel on it;
    turn from it and go on your way.
For they cannot sleep till they do evil;
        they are robbed of slumber till they make
            someone fall.
They eat the bread of wickedness
    and drink the wine of violence.

The path of the righteous is like the first gleam
            of dawn,
    shining ever brighter till the full light of day.
But the way of the wicked is like deep darkness;
    they do not know what makes them stumble.

My son, pay attention to what I say;
    listen closely to my words.
Do not let them out of your sight,
    keep them within your heart;
for they are life to those who find them
    and health to a man's whole body.
Above all else, guard your heart,
    for it is the wellspring of life.
Put away perversity from your mouth;
    keep corrupt talk far from your lips.
Let your eyes look straight ahead,
    fix your gaze directly before you.
Make level paths for your feet
    and take only ways that are firm.

Do not swerve to the right or the left;
    keep your foot from evil.

PROVERBS 4

As God's children, the best advice we can receive is to freely receive the best possible advice—that which comes from our Father. As a parent instills character in a child's heart through both teaching and example, so God instills wisdom within us when we open our hearts to learn of Him. His precepts and principles are always the source of protection, guidance, and love.

If parents dispense good advice to their children, how much more so the Father of all parents? The only question is, Are we willing to accept that advice? Are we as committed to that task as was the psalmist?

How can a young man keep his way pure?
    By living according to your word.
I seek you with all my heart;
    do not let me stray from your commands.
I have hidden your word in my heart
    that I might not sin against you.
Praise be to you, O LORD;
    teach me your decrees.
With my lips I recount
    all the laws that come from your mouth.
I rejoice in following your statutes
    as one rejoices in great riches.
I meditate on your precepts
    and consider your ways.
I delight in your decrees;
    I will not neglect your word.

PSALM 119:9-16

Teach me, O LORD, to follow your decrees;
    then I will keep them to the end.
Give me understanding, and I will keep your law
    and obey it with all my heart.
Direct me in the path of your commands,
    for there I find delight.
Turn my heart toward your statutes
    and not toward selfish gain.
Turn my eyes away from worthless things;
    preserve my life according to your word.
Fulfill your promise to your servant,
    so that you may be feared.
Take away the disgrace I dread,
    for your laws are good.
How I long for your precepts!
    Preserve my life in your righteousness.

PSALM 119:33-40

The Heart's Treasure-House

WHAT IS YOUR FAVORITE MEMORY VERSE? When did you first learn it? Why is it your favorite passage? Have you ever used it in a practical way—to overcome a temptation, to lift your spirit, to answer a false teaching?

The elders of Israel, to whom God entrusted His wisdom, knew that spiritual enemies confront us quickly. We seldom have time to plan a reasoned counterattack. Therefore they advise us to hold in readiness our defensive weapons—the lessons we have learned from Wisdom's teaching. Those lessons must be learned so well that we can use them on a moment's notice.

Repetition and memory serve a purpose. They keep Wisdom in our mind at all times. They enable us to trust in God's protection and live without fear of being overcome in our weakest moments.

Memory verses are not for children only. The older we get, the more we need the strength of God's Word in our minds. The best place to begin a ministry of memory is in Proverbs. And the best verse is the one that highlights this section: "The fear of the LORD is the beginning of knowledge."

The Importance of the Heart

The proverbs of Solomon son of David, king of Israel:

for attaining wisdom and discipline;
    for understanding words of insight;
for acquiring a disciplined and prudent life,
    doing what is right and just and fair;
for giving prudence to the simple,
    knowledge and discretion to the young—
let the wise listen and add to their learning,
    and let the discerning get guidance—
for understanding proverbs and parables,
    the sayings and riddles of the wise.

The fear of the LORD is the beginning of knowledge,
    but fools despise wisdom and discipline.

PROVERBS 1:1-7

Pay attention and listen to the sayings of the wise;
    apply your heart to what I teach,
for it is pleasing when you keep them in your heart
    and have all of them ready on your lips.
So that your trust may be in the LORD,
    I teach you today, even you.
Have I not written thirty sayings for you,
    sayings of counsel and knowledge,
teaching you true and reliable words,
    so that you can give sound answers
    to him who sent you?

PROVERBS 22:17-21

Psalms

BECAUSE THE HEART IS THE RESERVOIR OUT OF WHICH flow the issues, motives, and actions of life, we must be careful how we fill that reservoir. It is never empty. We will fill it either with truth and beauty or with evil and ugliness. The problem is that, inevitably, we attempt to fill it with both— or, at the very least, allow evil and ugliness to spill into it through benign neglect. When that happens, a divided heart is vulnerable to every onslaught imaginable. Hear now the prayer of David who, like ourselves, knew how terribly wrong everything can go when we don't give God our undivided attention.

Hear, O LORD, and answer me,
    for I am poor and needy.
Guard my life, for I am devoted to you.
    You are my God; save your servant
    who trusts in you.
Have mercy on me, O Lord,
    for I call to you all day long.
Bring joy to your servant,
    for to you, O Lord,
    I lift up my soul.

You are forgiving and good, O Lord,
    abounding in love to all who call to you.
Hear my prayer, O LORD;
    listen to my cry for mercy.
In the day of my trouble I will call to you,
    for you will answer me.

Among the gods there is none like you, O Lord;
    no deeds can compare with yours.

All the nations you have made
     will come and worship before you, O Lord;
     they will bring glory to your name.
For you are great and do marvelous deeds;
     you alone are God.

Teach me your way, O Lord,
     and I will walk in your truth;
give me an undivided heart,
     that I may fear your name.
I will praise you, O Lord my God, with all my heart;
     I will glorify your name forever.
For great is your love toward me;
     you have delivered me from the depths of the
          grave.

Psalm 86:1-13

Giving God Control

WHOM DO YOU TRUST—YOURSELF OR GOD? Who is ultimately in control of your life? Do you look for truth within yourself or in God? The real question is, Are you your own god?

Moses and the prophets condemned idolatry. We censure those who carve wooden gods or cast religious idols from precious metals. But an idol is anything we worship other than the God of heaven. Idolatry is giving top priority to anything or anyone other than God. We can become our own gods by giving ourselves preeminence.

The first problem with relying on ourselves is that we do not always know what is best for either ourselves or others. We are as blind to our needs as we are to our faults. We are deceived and arrogant if we think we can control our lives, much less our universe.

The second problem is that if we are at the controls, then God is not. And if God is not, then we assume God's responsibility for getting things right. Can we deliver? Do we want that responsibility?

The bad news is that we are not in charge. The good news is that God is in charge and that He is watching over all that we do. He cares what happens to us. He knows when we need His strength. He nudges nature on our behalf. Throughout our life, divine purpose prevails so that we are not victims of our own limited understanding.

The Fear of the Lord

The fear of the LORD is the beginning of wisdom,
and knowledge of the Holy One is understanding.
For through me your days will be many,
and years will be added to your life.
If you are wise, your wisdom will reward you:
if you are a mocker, you alone will suffer.

PROVERBS 9:10-12

The fear of the LORD adds length to life,
but the years of the wicked are cut short.

PROVERBS 10:27

He whose walk is upright fears the LORD,
but he whose ways are devious despises him.

PROVERBS 14:2

He who fears the LORD has a secure fortress,
and for his children it will be a refuge.
The fear of the LORD is a fountain of life,
turning a man from the snares of death.

PROVERBS 14:26-27

The fear of the LORD teaches a man wisdom,
and humility comes before honor.

PROVERBS 15:33

The fear of the LORD leads to life:
Then one rests content, untouched by trouble.

PROVERBS 19:23

Blessed is the man who always fears the LORD,
    but he who hardens his heart falls into trouble.

PROVERBS 28:14

Trust in God or Self

Trust in the LORD with all your heart
    and lean not on your own understanding;
in all your ways acknowledge him,
    and he will make your paths straight.

Do not be wise in your own eyes;
    fear the LORD and shun evil.
This will bring health to your body
    and nourishment to your bones.

PROVERBS 3:5-8

There is a way that seems right to a man,
    but in the end it leads to death.

PROVERBS 14:12; 16:25

Commit to the LORD whatever you do,
    and your plans will succeed.

PROVERBS 16:3

Whoever gives heed to instruction prospers,
    and blessed is he who trusts in the LORD.

PROVERBS 16:20

A fool finds no pleasure in understanding
    but delights in airing his own opinions.

PROVERBS 18:2

The words of a man's mouth are deep waters,
    but the fountain of wisdom is a bubbling brook.

PROVERBS 18:4

The name of the LORD is a strong tower;
the righteous run to it and are safe.

PROVERBS 18:10

A man's own folly ruins his life,
yet his heart rages against the LORD.

PROVERBS 19:3

A man's steps are directed by the LORD.
How then can anyone understand his own way?

PROVERBS 20:24

A wise man attacks the city of the mighty
and pulls down the stronghold in which
they trust.

PROVERBS 21:22

Do you see a man wise in his own eyes?
There is more hope for a fool than for him.

PROVERBS 26:12

He who trusts in himself is a fool,
but he who walks in wisdom is kept safe.

PROVERBS 28:26

Fear of man will prove to be a snare,
but whoever trusts in the LORD is kept safe.

PROVERBS 29:25

Divine Providence

The eyes of the LORD are everywhere,
keeping watch on the wicked and the good.

PROVERBS 15:3

To man belong the plans of the heart,
> but from the LORD comes the reply of the tongue.
>> PROVERBS 16:1

The LORD works out everything for his own ends—
> even the wicked for a day of disaster.
>> Proverbs 16:4

In his heart a man plans his course,
> but the LORD determines his steps.
>> PROVERBS 16:9

The lot is cast into the lap,
> but its every decision is from the LORD.
>> PROVERBS 16:33

Many are the plans in a man's heart,
> but it is the LORD's purpose that prevails.
>> PROVERBS 19:21

There is no wisdom, no insight, no plan
> that can succeed against the LORD.

The horse is made ready for the day of battle,
> but victory rests with the LORD.
>> PROVERBS 21:30-31

The eyes of the LORD keep watch over knowledge,
> but he frustrates the words of the unfaithful.
>> PROVERBS 22:12

Do not boast about tomorrow,
> for you do not know what a day may bring forth.
>> PROVERBS 27:1

Psalms

Many of us have a problem with the idea of fearing the Lord. We try in vain to redefine fear as "reverence" or "respect," or perhaps simply humility in the presence of a God who evokes great awe. But love and genuine fear are not antithetical to each other. A child who basks in the love of his parents deservedly fears the consequences of having broken the cookie jar, which was strictly off-limits. Only a truly fearful God can defend us against all the evil things in our life over which we are helpless.

Oh, for a heart that knows whom to fear most and knows that—because of Him—there is nothing to fear!

Praise the Lord.

I will extol the Lord with all my heart
    in the council of the upright and in the assembly.

Great are the works of the Lord;
    they are pondered by all who delight in them.
Glorious and majestic are his deeds,
    and his righteousness endures forever.
He has caused his wonders to be remembered;
    the Lord is gracious and compassionate.
He provides food for those who fear him;
    he remembers his covenant forever.
He has shown his people the power of his works,
    giving them the lands of other nations.
The works of his hands are faithful and just;
    all his precepts are trustworthy.
They are steadfast for ever and ever,
    done in faithfulness and uprightness.

He provided redemption for his people;
    he ordained his covenant forever—
    holy and awesome is his name.

The fear of the LORD is the beginning of wisdom;
    all who follow his precepts have good
        understanding.
    To him belongs eternal praise.

PSALM 111

Trusting God's Guidance

Have you ever tried to fix something, only to make it worse? Did you ever assemble a toy on Christmas Eve, only to discover that you had left out an important step? How many times have you ignored the instruction manual or refused to read the directions that came in the box? Have you watched with amazement as an expert quickly performed what you assumed to be a complicated task? While do-it-yourselfers deserve an "A" for effort, some stubbornly refuse to admit their failure. Only a fool would dare to assume he can understand everything on his own. A wise person turns to a source of help when it is needed.

Life is like that. Some people realize that life is more than nine-to-five. They are motivated by a higher meaning or purpose. Most of us, however, go along, day by day, year by year, doing what comes easily. If something appears to work, it is good enough. We should not be surprised that our lives are broken or that we realize at the end of life that we have left out important steps.

Have you discovered God's purpose for your life, or are you just going along? Do you regularly read God's Instruction Manual, or does it gather dust while you wonder what happened to your life?

Failing to trust God's guidance usually means that we think we can make do on our own—that we are self-sufficient. For most of us, the idea that we need only look within ourselves for guidance is a matter of foolish pride. When we find ourselves in trouble, to whom do we turn? To ourselves? In times of disaster, suffering, and heartache, do we not intuitively seek guidance from One far greater than ourselves?

If we can turn to God in times of trouble, surely that same God is able to enrich our lives when times are good. Even if we could somehow manage on our own, might we manage even better by seeking the advice and wisdom of the One who made us? Surely He must know what kind of life will bring out the best in us.

And if personal pride is important to us, then why not put it to work in a positive way? By choosing to follow God's superior guidance, we can be justly proud of having the good sense to know what is best for our lives. When others see what our insightful decision has done for us, they may even be envious!

Wisdom and Folly

The teaching of the wise is a fountain of life,
    turning a man from the snares of death.

PROVERBS 13:14

The wealth of the wise is their crown,
    but the folly of fools yields folly.

PROVERBS 14:24

The path of life leads upward for the wise
    to keep him from going down to the grave.

PROVERBS 15:24

Understanding is a fountain of life to those who
         have it,
     but folly brings punishment to fools.

                                    PROVERBS 16:22

Better to meet a bear robbed of her cubs
     than a fool in his folly.

                                    PROVERBS 17:12

Wisdom is too high for a fool;
     in the assembly at the gate he has nothing to say.
                                    PROVERBS 24:7

Eat honey, my son, for it is good;
     honey from the comb is sweet to your taste.
Know also that wisdom is sweet to your soul;
     if you find it, there is a future hope for you,
     and your hope will not be cut off.

                                    PROVERBS 24:13-14

Dealing with Fools

Do not answer a fool according to his folly,
     or you will be like him yourself.

Answer a fool according to his folly,
     or he will be wise in his own eyes.

Like cutting off one's feet or drinking violence
     is the sending of a message by the hand of a fool.

Like a lame man's legs that hang limp
     is a proverb in the mouth of a fool.

Like tying a stone in a sling
     is the giving of honor to a fool.

Like a thornbush in a drunkard's hand
    is a proverb in the mouth of a fool.

Like an archer who wounds at random
    is he who hires a fool or any passer-by.

As a dog returns to its vomit,
    so a fool repeats his folly.

Proverbs 26:4-11

Though you grind a fool in a mortar,
    grinding him like grain with a pestle,
    you will not remove his folly from him.

Proverbs 27:22

If a wise man goes to court with a fool,
    the fool rages and scoffs, and there is no peace.

Proverbs 29:9

Discernment and Understanding

Wisdom is found on the lips of the discerning,
    but a rod is for the back of him who lacks
        judgment.

Proverbs 10:13

A fool finds pleasure in evil conduct,
    but a man of understanding delights in wisdom.

Proverbs 10:23

Good understanding wins favor,
    but the way of the unfaithful is hard.

Proverbs 13:15

The mocker seeks wisdom and finds none,
    but knowledge comes easily to the discerning.

Proverbs 14:6

The wisdom of the prudent is to give thought to their
ways,
but the folly of fools is deception.

PROVERBS 14:8

A simple man believes anything,
but a prudent man gives thought to his steps.

PROVERBS 14:15

Wisdom reposes in the heart of the discerning
and even among fools she lets herself be known.

PROVERBS 14:33

Folly delights a man who lacks judgment,
but a man of understanding keeps a straight
course.

PROVERBS 15:21

How much better to get wisdom than gold,
to choose understanding rather than silver!

PROVERBS 16:16

A discerning man keeps wisdom in view,
but a fool's eyes wander to the ends of the earth.

PROVERBS 17:24

He who gets wisdom loves his own soul;
he who cherishes understanding prospers.

PROVERBS 19:8

The purposes of a man's heart are deep waters,
but a man of understanding draws them out.

PROVERBS 20:5

Ears that hear and eyes that see—
the LORD has made them both.

PROVERBS 20:12

Knowledge

Wise men store up knowledge,
but the mouth of a fool invites ruin.

Proverbs 10:14

Every prudent man acts out of knowledge,
but a fool exposes his folly.

Proverbs 13:16

The simple inherit folly,
but the prudent are crowned with knowledge.

Proverbs 14:18

The discerning heart seeks knowledge,
but the mouth of a fool feeds on folly.

Proverbs 15:14

The heart of the discerning acquires knowledge;
the ears of the wise seek it out.

Proverbs 18:15

It is not good to have zeal without knowledge,
nor to be hasty and miss the way.

Proverbs 19:2

Gold there is, and rubies in abundance,
but lips that speak knowledge are a rare jewel.

Proverbs 20:15

When a mocker is punished, the simple gain wisdom;
when a wise man is instructed, he gets knowledge.

Proverbs 21:11

Apply your heart to instruction
and your ears to words of knowledge.

Proverbs 23:12

By wisdom a house is built,
    and through understanding it is established;
through knowledge its rooms are filled
    with rare and beautiful treasures.

PROVERBS 24:3-4

Psalms

IF THE CONSTRUCTION OF A GRAND HOUSE IS evidence of intelligent and wise planning, how much more so the creation of the universe? Of all mansions, the glorious home of man is supremely grand. Both day and night the vast universe stands ready to remind us that its architect and builder is the same knowledgeable and wise Maker who has brought each one of us into existence.

When we see the most far-flung stars and the tiniest subatomic particles faithfully following their Creator's laws, the precepts He has laid down for you and for me must surely take on added significance. Following our own lead and not seeking out our Maker's understanding of what constitutes a life well lived is the utmost folly.

Praise the LORD.

Praise the LORD from the heavens,
    praise him in the heights above.
Praise him, all his angels,
    praise him, all his heavenly hosts.
Praise him, sun and moon,
    praise him, all you shining stars.
Praise him, you highest heavens
    and you waters above the skies.
Let them praise the name of the LORD,
    for he commanded and they were created.

He set them in place for ever and ever;
    he gave a decree that will never pass away.
Praise the Lord from the earth,
    you great sea creatures and all ocean depths,
lightning and hail, snow and clouds,
    stormy winds that do his bidding,
you mountains and all hills,
    fruit trees and all cedars,
wild animals and all cattle,
    small creatures and flying birds,
kings of the earth and all nations,
    you princes and all rulers on earth,
young men and maidens,
    old men and children.

Let them praise the name of the Lord,
    for his name alone is exalted;
    his splendor is above the earth and the heavens.
He has raised up for his people a horn,
    the praise of all his saints,
    of Israel, the people close to his heart.

Praise the Lord.

Psalm 148

Giving and Taking Advice

We all hate to hear people say, "I told you so!" and see that glint of satisfaction in their eyes. We wonder if they weren't hoping we would fail so they would look good. Why did they warn us in the first place? What was their motive? Were they genuinely concerned about us?

Of course, sometimes an "I told you so" is in order. Why did we ignore the advice? Because of pride or undue haste? If so, we deserve our correction. Advice can be a precious gift. We ought to receive it appreciatively.

We may ignore good advice simply because of the source. Typically, we only accept advice if we respect the one who gives it. A true friend can get away with the most piercing of criticism. A stranger's advice should be discreet and cautious.

What does our experience in receiving advice tell us about giving it? It suggests that we ought to be selective. Solomon says that a good person will appreciate good advice, but a callous person will only resent us.

We also should first make sure we are truly a friend. Only through the door of trust will our advice be welcomed.

Advice and Rebuke

My son, do not forget my teaching,
    but keep my commands in your heart,
for they will prolong your life many years
    and bring you prosperity.

PROVERBS 3:1-2

Whoever corrects a mocker invites insult;
    whoever rebukes a wicked man incurs abuse.
Do not rebuke a mocker or he will hate you;
    rebuke a wise man and he will love you.
Instruct a wise man and he will be wiser still;
        teach a righteous man and he will add to his
            learning.

PROVERBS 9:7-9

The wise in heart accept commands,
    but a chattering fool comes to ruin.

PROVERBS 10:8

The way of a fool seems right to him,
    but a wise man listens to advice.

PROVERBS 12:15

A wise son heeds his father's instruction,
    but a mocker does not listen to rebuke.

PROVERBS 13:1

He who scorns instruction will pay for it,
    but he who respects a command is rewarded.

PROVERBS 13:13

He who listens to a life-giving rebuke
will be at home among the wise.

PROVERBS 15:31

A rebuke impresses a man of discernment
more than a hundred lashes a fool.

PROVERBS 17:10

He who obeys instructions guards his life,
but he who is contemptuous of his ways will die.

PROVERBS 19:16

Listen to advice and accept instruction,
and in the end you will be wise.

PROVERBS 19:20

Flog a mocker, and the simple will learn prudence;
rebuke a discerning man, and he will gain
knowledge.

PROVERBS 19:25

Stop listening to instruction, my son,
and you will stray from the words of knowledge.

PROVERBS 19:27

Do not speak to a fool,
for he will scorn the wisdom of your words.

PROVERBS 23:9

Like an earring of gold or an ornament of fine gold
is a wise man's rebuke to a listening ear.

PROVERBS 25:12

Better is open rebuke
than hidden love.

Wounds from a friend can be trusted,
　　but an enemy multiplies kisses.

PROVERBS 27:5-6

As iron sharpens iron,
　　so one man sharpens another.

PROVERBS 27:17

A man who remains stiff-necked after many rebukes
　　will suddenly be destroyed—without remedy.

PROVERBS 29:1

The Value of Advisors

For lack of guidance a nation falls,
　　but many advisers make victory sure.

PROVERBS 11:14

Plans fail for lack of counsel,
　　but with many advisers they succeed.

PROVERBS 15:22

Make plans by seeking advice;
　　if you wage war, obtain guidance.

PROVERBS 20:18

A wise man has great power,
　　and a man of knowledge increases strength;
for waging war you need guidance,
　　and for victory many advisers.

PROVERBS 24:5-6

Psalms

THE MATTER OF GIVING AND TAKING ADVICE hinges less on the content of the advice itself than on the attitude with which it is given or received. Even the best of advice can be dispensed with such arrogance that anyone on the receiving end would be warranted in closing his or her ears. On the other hand, the best-intended advice will be of no benefit to someone whose mind is already closed.

Like teaching a pig to sing, enlightening someone who shuns all advice is nearly impossible. So, take my advice: When God says, "Trust me," accept His words as the best advice you'll ever get.

> I will instruct you and teach you in the way you
>   should go;
>   I will counsel you and watch over you.
> Do not be like the horse or the mule,
>   which have no understanding
> but must be controlled by bit and bridle
>   or they will not come to you.
> Many are the woes of the wicked,
>   but the LORD's unfailing love
>   surrounds the man who trusts in him.
>
> Rejoice in the LORD and be glad, you righteous;
>   sing, all you who are upright in heart!
>   PSALM 32:8-11

Growth Through Discipline

Do YOUR CHILDHOOD MEMORIES INCLUDE A PARTICULAR switch or your father's belt? Do they include scenes of early discipline? Perhaps you only received a firm hand on the backside or a stern word of rebuke. It seemed so painful then—not so much the hurt itself but what it represented. It meant that our conduct had to be changed, that our attitude had to be more mature. There was a hierarchy of authority and a submission of wills—ours to our parents'.

Of course we never believed that discipline hurt our parents more than us. Nor did we appreciate the care and concern that prompted it. But now we understand. We don't dart into the street or stick our fingers into electrical sockets. Sometimes we share our possessions with other people even though we would like to keep them.

But we still fail to see the connection between discipline and growth. When God instructs us in our life, we rebel. When as a result we suffer or fall, we complain as if God were to blame. "Why is this happening to me?" we pout. "What kind of God would allow this to happen?" we demand.

Is discipline necessary only for children? Does it cause only them to grow? Have we nothing more to gain from it?

With children, discipline is rewarded by each new sign of maturity. We celebrate a banner day, for example, when a child says "I'm sorry" before he or she has to be reprimanded. As children of God, we show our spiritual maturity when we freely confess the sins we have committed, and the discipline of righteous struggle is rewarded with personal growth.

Proverbs

Discipline

My son, do not despise the LORD's discipline
    and do not resent his rebuke,
because the LORD disciplines those he loves,
    as a father the son he delights in.

PROVERBS 3:11-12

He who heeds discipline shows the way to life,
    but whoever ignores correction leads others astray.

PROVERBS 10:17

Whoever loves discipline loves knowledge,
    but he who hates correction is stupid.

PROVERBS 12:1

He who ignores discipline comes to poverty and
        shame,
    but whoever heeds correction is honored.

PROVERBS 13:18

He who spares the rod hates his son,
    but he who loves him is careful to discipline him.

PROVERBS 13:24

A fool spurns his father's discipline,
but whoever heeds correction shows prudence.
PROVERBS 15:5

Stern discipline awaits him who leaves the path;
he who hates correction will die.
PROVERBS 15:10

A mocker resents correction;
he will not consult the wise.
PROVERBS 15:12

He who ignores discipline despises himself,
but whoever heeds correction gains
understanding.
PROVERBS 15:32

Discipline your son, for in that there is hope;
do not be a willing party to his death.
PROVERBS 19:18

Blows and wounds cleanse away evil,
and beatings purge the inmost being.
PROVERBS 20:30

Train a child in the way he should go,
and when he is old he will not turn from it.
PROVERBS 22:6

Folly is bound up in the heart of a child,
but the rod of discipline will drive it far from him.
PROVERBS 22:15

Do not withhold discipline from a child;
if you punish him with the rod, he will not die.

Punish him with the rod
and save his soul from death

PROVERBS 23:13-14

The rod of correction imparts wisdom,
but a child left to himself disgraces his mother.

PROVERBS 29:15

Discipline your son, and he will give you peace;
he will bring delight to your soul.

PROVERBS 29:17

A servant cannot be corrected by mere words;
though he understands, he will not respond.

PROVERBS 29:19

If a man pampers his servant from youth,
he will bring grief in the end.

PROVERBS 29:21

Keeping the Law

Those who forsake the law praise the wicked,
but those who keep the law resist them.

PROVERBS 28:4

He who keeps the law is a discerning son,
but a companion of gluttons disgraces his father.

PROVERBS 28:7

If anyone turns a deaf ear to the law,
even his prayers are detestable.

PROVERBS 28:9

Where there is no revelation, the people cast off
restraint;
but blessed is he who keeps the law.

PROVERBS 29:18

Repentance

Fools mock at making amends for sin,
but good will is found among the upright.

PROVERBS 14:9

He who conceals his sins does not prosper,
but whoever confesses and renounces them finds
mercy.

PROVERBS 28:13

Psalms

DON'T YOU SIMPLY HATE THE THOUGHT of being disciplined?
Think about that music teacher who made you practice
the scales over and over, ad nauseam. Or the coach who
put you through seemingly endless drills until you were
ready to drop. Discipline wouldn't win many popular
elections! But the payoff is worth the effort.

Like eating our vegetables, discipline is always good
for us. Why? Because only through discipline are we
soundly taught. Ever consider the connection between *discipline* and *disciple*? They go together like horse and carriage, love and marriage. You can't have one without the
other.

Praise our God, O peoples,
let the sound of his praise be heard;

he has preserved our lives
    and kept our feet from slipping.
For you, O God, tested us;
    you refined us like silver.
You brought us into prison
    and laid burdens on our backs.
You let men ride over our heads;
    we went through fire and water,
    but you brought us to a place of abundance.

PSALM 66:8-12

Strength Through Righteous Living

W**HAT MAKES A NATION STRONG**? Is it military power, economic strength, or a particular form of government? Why is it that powerful nations have fallen and been forgotten? Many factors contribute to the rise and fall of nations. Among them, one thing seems certain: A wicked nation cannot remain strong. If it is not defeated by its enemies, it will collapse internally.

Because God personally rules over nations and their leaders, He can bring a nation to its knees. Even apart from that possibility, one thing is clear about the nature of evil: Evil bears the seeds of its own destruction. Wickedness hides a moral time bomb.

If a nation oppresses its people long enough, its citizens eventually will rebel. If a government starves its poor long enough, the hungry one day will revolt. A corrupt and immoral government walks the road of self-destruction.

By contrast, a righteous nation is bound to prosper because goodness bears the seed of its own reward. When citizens are treated justly, they respond with decency. When their labor is given incentive, they produce abundantly. When their safety is secure, they live peaceably and without complaint.

As with nations, so also with individuals: Goodness and evil each have inherent and distinctive consequences.

Righteousness and Wickedness

Blessings crown the head of the righteous,
>but violence overwhelms the mouth of the wicked.

The memory of the righteous will be a blessing,
>but the name of the wicked will rot.
>>PROVERBS 10:6-7

The wages of the righteous bring them life,
>but the income of the wicked brings them
>>punishment.
>>>PROVERBS 10:16

The prospect of the righteous is joy,
>but the hopes of the wicked come to nothing.

The way of the LORD is a refuge for the righteous,
>but it is the ruin of those who do evil.

The righteous will never be uprooted,
>but the wicked will not remain in the land.
>>PROVERBS 10:28-30

The righteousness of the blameless makes a straight
>>way for them,
>but the wicked are brought down by their own
>>wickedness.

The righteousness of the upright delivers them,
  but the unfaithful are trapped by evil desires.

When a wicked man dies, his hope perishes;
  all he expected from his power comes to nothing.

The righteous man is rescued from trouble,
  and it comes on the wicked instead.

With his mouth the godless destroys his neighbor,
  but through knowledge the righteous escape.

When the righteous prosper, the city rejoices;
  when the wicked perish, there are shouts of joy.
                                    PROVERBS 11:5-10

The wicked man earns deceptive wages,
  but he who sows righteousness reaps a sure
    reward.

The truly righteous man attains life,
  but he who pursues evil goes to his death.

The LORD detests men of perverse heart
  but he delights in those whose ways are blameless.
                                    PROVERBS 11:18-20

The desire of the righteous ends only in good,
  but the hope of the wicked only in wrath.
                                    PROVERBS 11:23

A good man obtains favor from the LORD,
  but the LORD condemns a crafty man.

A man cannot be established through wickedness,
  but the righteous cannot be uprooted.
                                    PROVERBS 12:2-3

The plans of the righteous are just,
    but the advice of the wicked is deceitful.

The words of the wicked lie in wait for blood,
    but the speech of the upright rescues them.

Wicked men are overthrown and are no more,
    but the house of the righteous stands firm.

A man is praised according to his wisdom,
    but men with warped minds are despised.

Proverbs 12:5-8

The wicked desire the plunder of evil men,
    but the root of the righteous flourishes.

Proverbs 12:12

No harm befalls the righteous,
    but the wicked have their fill of trouble.

Proverbs 12:21

In the way of righteousness there is life;
    along that path is immortality.

Proverbs 12:28

The light of the righteous shines brightly,
    but the lamp of the wicked is snuffed out.

Proverbs 13:9

Misfortune pursues the sinner,
    but prosperity is the reward of the righteous.

Proverbs 13:21

The righteous eat to their hearts' content,
    but the stomach of the wicked goes hungry.

Proverbs 13:25

The house of the wicked will be destroyed,
    but the tent of the upright will flourish.

PROVERBS 14:11

Evil men will bow down in the presence of the good,
    and the wicked at the gates of the righteous.

PROVERBS 14:19

Righteousness exalts a nation,
    but sin is a disgrace to any people.

PROVERBS 14:34

The house of the righteous contains great treasure,
    but the income of the wicked brings them trouble.

PROVERBS 15:6

The LORD detests the way of the wicked
    but he loves those who pursue righteousness.

PROVERBS 15:9

The righteous man leads a blameless life;
    blessed are his children after him.

PROVERBS 20:7

The wicked become a ransom for the righteous,
    and the unfaithful for the upright.

PROVERBS 21:18

Do not lie in wait like an outlaw against a righteous
        man's house,
    do not raid his dwelling place;
for though a righteous man falls seven times, he rises
        again,
    but the wicked are brought down by calamity.

PROVERBS 24:15-16

When the righteous triumph, there is great elation;
but when the wicked rise to power, men go into
hiding.

PROVERBS 28:12

When the wicked rise to power, people go into hiding;
but when the wicked perish, the righteous thrive.

PROVERBS 28:28

When the righteous thrive, the people rejoice;
when the wicked rule, the people groan.

PROVERBS 29:2

When the wicked thrive, so does sin,
but the righteous will see their downfall.

PROVERBS 29:16

The righteous detest the dishonest;
the wicked detest the upright.

PROVERBS 29:27

As with nations, so with individuals: Righteousness
bears sweet fruit, while wickedness spoils and decays.
The problem is that the fruits of righteousness can continue on long after the rot has set in. So it is that an individual's or a nation's prosperity is often deceptive. Like a
rotten board hidden behind a layer of paint, when it suddenly gives way, we are surprised.

To change the metaphor yet again, righteous roots
must remain intact. Cut flowers may be beautiful for a
time, but they quickly wither once they are cut off from
the source. Are "Christian nations"—even those with vast

resources and strong armies—immune from this funda-
mental law of nature? Are we, ourselves, immune?

> Sing joyfully to the LORD, you righteous;
>> it is fitting for the upright to praise him.
> Praise the LORD with the harp;
>> make music to him on the ten-stringed lyre.
> Sing to him a new song;
>> play skillfully, and shout for joy.

> For the word of the LORD is right and true;
>> he is faithful in all he does.
> The LORD loves righteousness and justice;
>> the earth is full of his unfailing love.

> By the word of the LORD were the heavens made,
>> their starry host by the breath of his mouth.
> He gathers the waters of the sea into jars;
>> he puts the deep into storehouses.
> Let all the earth fear the LORD;
>> let all the people of the world revere him.
> For he spoke, and it came to be;
>> he commanded, and it stood firm.
> The LORD foils the plans of the nations;
>> he thwarts the purposes of the peoples.
> But the plans of the LORD stand firm forever,
>> the purposes of his heart through all generations.

> Blessed is the nation whose God is the LORD,
>> the people he chose for his inheritance.
> From heaven the LORD looks down
>> and sees all mankind;
> from his dwelling place he watches
>> all who live on earth—
> he who forms the hearts of all,
>> who considers everything they do.

No king is saved by the size of his army;
    no warrior escapes by his great strength.
A horse is a vain hope for deliverance;
    despite all its great strength it cannot save.
But the eyes of the Lord are on those who fear him,
    on those whose hope is in his unfailing love,
to deliver them from death
    and keep them alive in famine.

We wait in hope for the Lord;
    he is our help and our shield.
In him our hearts rejoice,
    for we trust in his holy name.
May your unfailing love rest upon us, O Lord,
    even as we put our hope in you.

                                        Psalm 33

Lives of Integrity

HAVE YOU NOTICED THAT THE GOOD GUYS AND THE bad guys have switched hats? Black has become white, and white has become at least dark gray. Sexual conduct once universally condemned as immoral is now an accepted lifestyle. Once-profane words are on the lips of churchgoers. Formerly scandalous fashions are hanging in almost every closet.

Falling short of our standards is one thing; we all do. Abandoning those standards altogether is another thing. We should be shocked by how comfortably we redefine our moral standards, approving the plainly evil. Can Wisdom bring us life where truth is turned inside out?

Proverbs makes it clear: We reap what we sow. Certainly we can see temporary exceptions to the rule. Some people of perverse character live in luxury while some individuals of integrity literally starve to death. But the principle nevertheless stands even if worldly circumstances do not always reflect it. Right living brings a fullness to life, whatever our circumstances. Moral perversion brings only grief.

This is true for a good reason: The God who made us is the One who gave us our basic moral standards. Because He made us, He knows how we should live to achieve our fullest potential. He also knows what will detract from our happiness. When we pervert His standards, we should expect to be unhappy. When we adhere to them faithfully, we are assured of rich blessings.

Integrity and Perversion

The man of integrity walks securely,
  but he who takes crooked paths will be found out.
  Proverbs 10:9

Righteousness guards the man of integrity,
  but wickedness overthrows the sinner.
  Proverbs 13:6

The Lord detests the thoughts of the wicked,
  but those of the pure are pleasing to him.
  Proverbs 15:26

The way of the guilty is devious,
  but the conduct of the innocent is upright.
  Proverbs 21:8

He who plots evil
  will be known as a schemer.
The schemes of folly are sin,
  and men detest a mocker.
  Proverbs 24:8-9

He whose walk is blameless is kept safe,
  but he whose ways are perverse will suddenly fall.
  Proverbs 28:18

Bloodthirsty men hate a man of integrity
and seek to kill the upright.

PROVERBS 29:10

Appropriate Consequences

The LORD's curse is on the house of the wicked,
but he blesses the home of the righteous.
He mocks proud mockers
but gives grace to the humble.
The wise inherit honor,
but fools he holds up to shame.

PROVERBS 3:33-35

The LORD does not let the righteous go hungry
but he thwarts the craving of the wicked.

PROVERBS 10:3

The blessing of the LORD brings wealth,
and he adds no trouble to it.

PROVERBS 10:22

What the wicked dreads will overtake him;
what the righteous desire will be granted.
When the storm has swept by, the wicked are gone,
but the righteous stand firm forever.

PROVERBS 10:24-25

Be sure of this: The wicked will not go unpunished,
but those who are righteous will go free.

PROVERBS 11:21

He who seeks good finds good will,
but evil comes to him who searches for it.

PROVERBS 11:27

The fruit of the righteous is a tree of life,
and he who wins souls is wise.

If the righteous receive their due on earth,
how much more the ungodly and the sinner!

Proverbs 11:30-31

The faithless will be fully repaid for their ways,
and the good man rewarded for his.

Proverbs 14:14

Do not those who plot evil go astray?
But those who plan what is good find love and
faithfulness.

Proverbs 14:22

When a man's ways are pleasing to the Lord,
He makes even his enemies live at peace with him.

Proverbs 16:7

If a man pays back evil for good,
evil will never leave his house.

Proverbs 17:13

When wickedness comes, so does contempt,
and with shame comes disgrace.

Proverbs 18:3

Penalties are prepared for mockers,
and beatings for the backs of fools.

Proverbs 19:29

The Righteous One takes note of the house of the
wicked
and brings the wicked to ruin.

Proverbs 21:12

A man who strays from the path of understanding
    comes to rest in the company of the dead.
                                   PROVERBS 21:16

He who pursues righteousness and love
    finds life, prosperity and honor.
                                     PROVERBS 21:21

He who sows wickedness reaps trouble,
    and the rod of his fury will be destroyed.
                                     PROVERBS 22:8

Like snow in summer or rain in harvest,
    honor is not fitting for a fool.
                                     PROVERBS 26:1

A whip for the horse, a halter for the donkey,
    and a rod for the backs of fools!
                                     PROVERBS 26:3

If a man digs a pit, he will fall into it;
    if a man rolls a stone, it will roll back on him.
                                     PROVERBS 26:27

Psalms

WE LIVE IN A WORLD THAT SEEKS TO BE GUILT FREE and consequence free, and all the more so, it seems, with the rise of shameless, socially condoned perversion. Sadder still is the arrogance that boasts of that perversion and is blind to its inevitable consequences. At no time in recent memory have David's words painted so familiar a picture: "The wicked freely strut about when what is vile is honored among men."

Integrity is not simply a matter of being honest. Integrity is drawing a clear line between good and evil. When that line is blurred beyond recognition, we have become like God (or so we think), knowing good and evil as we want to know it. David lamented the perversion of saying, "We own our lips—who is our master?" Today's popular mantras are no better: "Have it your way," "Just do it!" and that ultimately dismissive "Whatever…"

Help, LORD, for the godly are no more;
    the faithful have vanished from among men.
Everyone lies to his neighbor;
    their flattering lips speak with deception.

May the LORD cut off all flattering lips
    and every boastful tongue
that says, "We will triumph with our tongues;
    we own our lips—who is our master?"

"Because of the oppression of the weak
    and the groaning of the needy,
I will now arise," says the LORD.
    "I will protect them from those who malign them."
And the words of the LORD are flawless,
    like silver refined in a furnace of clay,
    purified seven times.

O LORD, you will keep us safe
    and protect us from such people forever.
The wicked freely strut about
    when what is vile is honored among men.

PSALM 12

Serving with Sincerity

HAVE YOU EVER SAT THROUGH A SERMON WITHOUT hearing a word of it? Have you partaken of communion while thinking ahead to lunch? Have you given a gift, hoping that you would get a favor in return? When someone has paid you a compliment, have you jokingly asked him what he wanted?

On one level our motives do not matter. The reason we stop when the light turns red may be habit, good citizenship, practical precaution, or only because someone we respect or fear is watching us. Whatever our reason, what matters is that we stop. On another level our motives are extremely important. If we shoot at a person in self-defense, the law will not hold us accountable. If we shoot with malicious intent, we will find ourselves behind bars.

When someone does us a favor, we should not question what prompted their generosity. When someone asks for forgiveness, we would be wrong to assume that he is only trying to avoid punishment or revenge. Rarely can we know a person's heart. Besides, we often act because of more than one motivation, and sometimes we may not know exactly what impels us.

God, however, knows our hearts and is concerned with the motives behind our conduct. We receive no credit for good deeds done from evil intent. The prophets remind us frequently that God hates false worship! He might prefer that we stay at home rather than go insincerely through the motions of a formal worship service. Even when we worship sincerely on Sunday, we can sin by acting unjustly toward other people during the week.

Wisdom teaches us to be consistent in thought, word, and deed: We avoid the sham of pretense, we safeguard the trust of those who rely on our word, and we achieve peace of mind through an inner harmony.

Motive and the Heart

Death and Destruction lie open before the Lord—
how much more the hearts of men!
Proverbs 15:11

All a man's ways seem innocent to him,
but motives are weighed by the Lord.
Proverbs 16:2

The crucible for silver and the furnace for gold,
but the Lord tests the heart.
Proverbs 17:3

Even a child is known by his actions,
by whether his conduct is pure and right.
Proverbs 20:11

The lamp of the Lord searches the spirit of a man;
it searches out his inmost being.
Proverbs 20:27

All a man's ways seem right to him,
  but the LORD weighs the heart.

PROVERBS 21:2

As water reflects a face,
  so a man's heart reflects the man.

PROVERBS 27:19

False Worship

The LORD detests the sacrifice of the wicked,
  but the prayer of the upright pleases him.

PROVERBS 15:8

The LORD is far from the wicked
  but he hears the prayer of the righteous.

PROVERBS 15:29

To do what is right and just
  is more acceptable to the LORD than sacrifice.

PROVERBS 21:3

The sacrifice of the wicked is detestable—
  how much more so when brought with evil intent?

PROVERBS 21:27

Duplicity

A scoundrel and villain,
    who goes about with a corrupt mouth,
    who winks with his eye,
    signals with his feet
    and motions with his fingers,
    who plots evil with deceit in his heart—
    he always stirs up dissension.

Therefore disaster will overtake him in an instant;
    he will suddenly be destroyed—without remedy.
        Proverbs 6:12-15

He who winks maliciously causes grief,
    and a chattering fool comes to ruin.

The mouth of the righteous is a fountain of life,
    but violence overwhelms the mouth of the wicked.
        Proverbs 10:10-11

The integrity of the upright guides them,
    but the unfaithful are destroyed by their duplicity.
        Proverbs 11:3

He who winks with his eye is plotting perversity;
    he who purses his lips is bent on evil.
        Proverbs 16:30

"It's no good, it's no good!" says the buyer;
    then off he goes and boasts about his purchase.
        Proverbs 20:14

Do not eat the food of a stingy man,
    do not crave his delicacies;
for he is the kind of man
    who is always thinking about the cost.
"Eat and drink," he says to you,
    but his heart is not with you.
You will vomit up the little you have eaten
    and will have wasted your compliments.
        Proverbs 23:6-8

Like a coating of glaze over earthenware
    are fervent lips with an evil heart.

A malicious man disguises himself with his lips,
>   but in his heart he harbors deceit.
Though his speech is charming, do not believe him,
>   for seven abominations fill his heart.
His malice may be concealed by deception,
>   but his wickedness will be exposed in the
>   assembly.

PROVERBS 26:23-26

Psalms

DECEPTION, DUPLICITY, AND INSINCERE WORSHIP...they each include a disconnection between one's acts and one's heart. In psychological terms, we would call it schizophrenia. We might expect such insincerity on the part of those who are patently unrighteous, but God undoubtedly abhors duplicity on the part of those who make a pretense of being righteous. Or is that the very problem—pretense?

In the following psalm, Asaph warns that God is calling His own covenant people to account for living inconsistently with the sacrifices they bring before Him. What God desires most is that we, His covenant people, live consistently with the faith we profess. Honoring God in that way sends up a sweeter aroma than any sacrifice we might bring.

The Mighty One, God, the LORD,
>   speaks and summons the earth
>   from the rising of the sun to the place where it sets.
From Zion, perfect in beauty,
>   God shines forth.
Our God comes and will not be silent;
>   a fire devours before him,

and around him a tempest rages.
He summons the heavens above,
 and the earth, that he may judge his people:
"Gather to me my consecrated ones,
 who made a covenant with me by sacrifice."
And the heavens proclaim his righteousness,
 for God himself is judge.

         Selah

"Hear, O my people, and I will speak,
 O Israel, and I will testify against you:
 I am God, your God.
I do not rebuke you for your sacrifices
 or your burnt offerings, which are ever before me.
I have no need of a bull from your stall
 or of goats from your pens,
for every animal of the forest is mine,
 and the cattle on a thousand hills.
I know every bird in the mountains,
 and the creatures of the field are mine.
If I were hungry I would not tell you,
 for the world is mine, and all that is in it.
Do I eat the flesh of bulls
 or drink the blood of goats?
Sacrifice thank offerings to God,
 fulfill your vows to the Most High,
and call upon me in the day of trouble;
 I will deliver you, and you will honor me."

But to the wicked, God says:

"What right have you to recite my laws
 or take my covenant on your lips?
You hate my instruction
 and cast my words behind you.

SERVING WITH SINCERITY

When you see a thief, you join with him;
   you throw in your lot with adulterers.
You use your mouth for evil
   and harness your tongue to deceit.
You speak continually against your brother
   and slander your own mother's son.
These things you have done and I kept silent;
   you thought I was altogether like you.
But I will rebuke you
   and accuse you to your face.

"Consider this, you who forget God,
   or I will tear you to pieces, with none to rescue:
He who sacrifices thank offerings honors me,
   and he prepares the way
   so that I may show him the salvation of God."

PSALM 50

Choosing to Love

How do you know if someone really loves you? How do you know if you love someone else? These questions usually are associated with romantic love. But we are told that we are to love even our enemies. How can we ever love any enemy? How can we love those whom we don't personally care for? Why should we want to?

Faithfulness to a relationship is an attribute of love because it builds trust. Trust maintains a steady course while feelings of love flutter in the breeze. Trust allows us to think kindly of someone we may not like at the moment. Not surprisingly, we trust those whom we love. The surprise is that we grow to love those whom we are willing to trust—even those we might not like initially.

Love can result from conscious choice. It comes when we choose to treat our enemy as a friend, when we choose not to be delighted when he encounters trouble, when we choose to say something friendly rather than something abusive or to ignore him completely.

Who is the winner when we love an enemy? Both parties, of course. The "enemy" usually responds well to the unexpected acceptance, and we feel warmed for responding properly. If we previously had a history of mutual hatred or heaping mounds of dislike, we feel great relief from all the guilt and alienation. In this case, "doing unto others" means doing something nice for ourselves as well.

Love and Faithfulness

Let love and faithfulness never leave you;
    bind them around your neck,
    write them on the tablet of your heart.
Then you will win favor and a good name
    in the sight of God and man.

PROVERBS 3:3-4

Through love and faithfulness sin is atoned for;
    through the fear of the LORD a man avoids evil.

PROVERBS 16:6

Many a man claims to have unfailing love,
    but a faithful man who can find?

PROVERBS 20:6

Like a bad tooth or a lame foot
    is reliance on the unfaithful in times of trouble.

PROVERBS 25:19

Love, Hatred, and Compassion

Hatred stirs up dissension,
    but love covers over all wrongs.

PROVERBS 10:12

Better a meal of vegetables where there is love
    than a fattened calf with hatred.

PROVERBS 15:17

He who mocks the poor shows contempt for their
Maker;
whoever gloats over disaster will not go
unpunished.

PROVERBS 17:5

Do not gloat when your enemy falls;
when he stumbles, do not let your heart rejoice,
or the LORD will see and disapprove
and turn his wrath away from him.

PROVERBS 24:17-18

If your enemy is hungry, give him food to eat;
if he is thirsty, give him water to drink.
In doing this, you will heap burning coals on his head,
and the LORD will reward you.

PROVERBS 25:21-22

Kindness and Mercy

A kindhearted woman gains respect,
but ruthless men gain only wealth.

A kind man benefits himself,
but a cruel man brings trouble on himself.

PROVERBS 11:16-17

A righteous man cares for the needs of his animal,
but the kindest acts of the wicked are cruel.

PROVERBS 12:10

An anxious heart weighs a man down,
but a kind word cheers him up.

PROVERBS 12:25

The wicked man craves evil;
> his neighbor gets no mercy from him.

PROVERBS 21:10

Overstaying Welcome

If you find honey, eat just enough—
> too much of it, and you will vomit.
Seldom set foot in your neighbor's house—
> too much of you, and he will hate you.

PROVERBS 25:16-17

Psalms

IN A WORLD OF OVER-ROMANTICIZED LOVE where loving others rarely includes reaching out to the unlovable, God breaks through to remind us how much He loves us even when we disappoint Him over and over again. Rather than treat us as we deserve, He extends mercy and grace to recalcitrant sinners like you and me. If God Himself has chosen to love us, how can we choose not to love others around us?

But how does God love the unlovable, you ask? By remembering that we are dust, says David, who himself was not always willing to extend love and mercy to his enemies. Perhaps, along with David, we should look more closely at the unlovable. Every one of them seems to have more than a smudge of dust on their shoulders...not unlike ourselves!

Praise the LORD, O my soul;
> all my inmost being, praise his holy name.
Praise the LORD, O my soul,

and forget not all his benefits—
who forgives all your sins
and heals all your diseases,
who redeems your life from the pit
and crowns you with love and compassion,
who satisfies your desires with good things
so that your youth is renewed like the eagle's.

The LORD works righteousness
and justice for all the oppressed.

He made known his ways to Moses,
his deeds to the people of Israel:
The LORD is compassionate and gracious,
slow to anger, abounding in love.
He will not always accuse,
nor will he harbor his anger forever;
he does not treat us as our sins deserve
or repay us according to our iniquities.
For as high as the heavens are above the earth,
so great is his love for those who fear him;
as far as the east is from the west,
so far has he removed our transgressions from us.
As a father has compassion on his children,
so the LORD has compassion on those who fear
him;
for he knows how we are formed,
he remembers that we are dust.
As for man, his days are like grass,
he flourishes like a flower of the field;
the wind blows over it and it is gone,
and its place remembers it no more.
But from everlasting to everlasting
the LORD's love is with those who fear him,

and his righteousness with their children's
children—
with those who keep his covenant
and remember to obey his precepts.

The Lord has established his throne in heaven,
and his kingdom rules over all.

Praise the Lord, you his angels,
you mighty ones who do his bidding,
who obey his word.
Praise the Lord, all his heavenly hosts,
you his servants who do his will.
Praise the Lord, all his works
everywhere in his dominion.

Praise the Lord, O my soul.

Psalm 103

Selfish Self-Destruction

Who is the person you have the most difficulty liking? Have you ever asked yourself why you dislike that particular person? Did he or she do something to harm or annoy you? Or is this just a difficult person?

The person you identified may be unusually self-centered. He or she may lack humility or be selfish or greedy. Your nominee is also likely to be the jealous type. Jealousy is, after all, selfishness applied to relationships. Pickiness and quarreling are common traits. Does your candidate fit this picture?

We may actually like another person despite their being physically unattractive, or at a different educational level, or richer or poorer than we, or of another race or social class. None of these factors uniformly decide whom we may like or dislike. We normally like those who like us. We like those who treat us as equals, who believe that we are important and valuable. We like people who respect our ideas and beliefs, who help meet our needs.

The self-centered individual is the one who is difficult to like. He is so concerned about his own little world that no one else matters. He is not a team player. He puts his own needs ahead of other people's needs. He does not sacrifice. He does not compromise. In pretending to be greater than he is, he deceives only himself, not realizing his own faults.

When self-concern becomes so consuming, we find such a person unlikable. But to what extent are we that person? Do we know people who don't like us? Have we asked ourselves why they don't? Perhaps we need to have a talk with ourself. Who knows—it may be a conversation with someone we think very highly of!

Pride and Humility

When pride comes, then comes disgrace,
  but with humility comes wisdom.

PROVERBS 11:2

Better to be a nobody and yet have a servant
  than pretend to be somebody and have no food.

PROVERBS 12:9

One man pretends to be rich, yet has nothing;
  another pretends to be poor, yet has great wealth.

PROVERBS 13:7

Pride only breeds quarrels,
  but wisdom is found in those who take advice.

PROVERBS 13:10

The LORD tears down the proud man's house
  but he keeps the widow's boundaries intact.

PROVERBS 15:25

The LORD detests all the proud of heart.
  Be sure of this: They will not go unpunished.

PROVERBS 16:5

Pride goes before destruction,
    a haughty spirit before a fall.

Better to be lowly in spirit and among the oppressed
    than to share plunder with the proud.

PROVERBS 16:18-19

Before his downfall a man's heart is proud,
    but humility comes before honor.

PROVERBS 18:12

It is not fitting for a fool to live in luxury—
    how much worse for a slave to rule over princes!

PROVERBS 19:10

Who can say, "I have kept my heart pure;
    I am clean and without sin"?

PROVERBS 20:9

Haughty eyes and a proud heart,
    the lamp of the wicked, are sin!

PROVERBS 21:4

The proud and arrogant man—"Mocker" is his name;
    he behaves with overweening pride.

PROVERBS 21:24

Humility and the fear of the LORD
    bring wealth and honor and life.

PROVERBS 22:4

It is not good to eat too much honey,
    nor is it honorable to seek one's own honor.

PROVERBS 25:27

The sluggard is wiser in his own eyes
    than seven men who answer discreetly.

PROVERBS 26:16

Let another praise you, and not your own mouth,
someone else, and not your own lips.

PROVERBS 27:2

The crucible for silver and the furnace for gold,
but man is tested by the praise he receives.

PROVERBS 27:21

A man's pride brings him low,
but a man of lowly spirit gains honor.

PROVERBS 29:23

Selfishness

An unfriendly man pursues selfish ends;
he defies all sound judgment.

PROVERBS 18:1

Jealousy

Anger is cruel and fury overwhelming,
but who can stand before jealousy?

PROVERBS 27:4

Envy

A heart at peace gives life to the body,
but envy rots the bones.

PROVERBS 14:30

Do not fret because of evil men
or be envious of the wicked,
for the evil man has no future hope,
and the lamp of the wicked will be snuffed out.

PROVERBS 24:19-20

Greed

> A greedy man stirs up dissension,
>> but he who trusts in the LORD will prosper.
>>
>> PROVERBS 28:25

Psalms

WHAT LIES BEHIND VIRTUALLY EVERY VICE AND SIN? An exaggerated sense of one's self. To put one's own wishes and desires ahead of others is to be greedy, envious, jealous, and selfish. People often say that pride goes before a fall. Actually, the proverb tells us that a haughty spirit goes before a fall and pride goes before destruction. In a downward spiral leading from self to pride to haughty arrogance, this moral regression finally ends up declaring that God will not call the self-focused person to account. Once that delusion sets in, any evil can be contemplated.

Show me a self-centered person, and I'll show you trouble ahead. What should this say to parents who turn a blind eye and allow their children to be self-willed?

> Why, O LORD, do you stand far off?
>> Why do you hide yourself in times of trouble?

> In his arrogance the wicked man hunts down
>> the weak,
>> who are caught in the schemes he devises.
> He boasts of the cravings of his heart;
>> he blesses the greedy and reviles the LORD.
> In his pride the wicked does not seek him;
>> in all his thoughts there is no room for God.
> His ways are always prosperous;
>> he is haughty and your laws are far from him;
>> he sneers at all his enemies.

He says to himself, "Nothing will shake me;
    I'll always be happy and never have trouble."
His mouth is full of curses and lies and threats;
    trouble and evil are under his tongue.
He lies in wait near the villages;
    from ambush he murders the innocent,
    watching in secret for his victims.
He lies in wait like a lion in cover;
    he lies in wait to catch the helpless;
    he catches the helpless and drags them off in
        his net.
His victims are crushed, they collapse;
    they fall under his strength.
He says to himself, "God has forgotten;
    he covers his face and never sees."

Arise, Lord! Lift up your hand, O God.
    Do not forget the helpless.
Why does the wicked man revile God?
    Why does he say to himself,
    "He won't call me to account"?
But you, O God, do see trouble and grief;
    you consider it to take it in hand.
The victim commits himself to you;
    you are the helper of the fatherless.
Break the arm of the wicked and evil man;
    call him to account for his wickedness
    that would not be found out.

The Lord is King for ever and ever;
    the nations will perish from his land.
You hear, O Lord, the desire of the afflicted;
    you encourage them, and you listen to their cry,
defending the fatherless and the oppressed,
    in order that man, who is of the earth, may terrify
        no more.

Psalm 10

Freedom Through Self-Control

How strong is your willpower? Can you stick with a diet or get up early to run laps? Do you maintain daily quiet times or read your Bible regularly? What bad habit have you broken lately? Is your temper usually under control? When a child asks the same question for the fifth time, do you still have patience?

Most of us would rather tame a herd of wild stallions than ourselves. We can control corporations, budgets, employees, children, dinner parties, and virtually anything else. But controlling ourselves is the great challenge. Why is that?

Why do we hear ourselves yelling at other people without intending to? Why do we look at the empty candy box as if someone forced us to eat the entire contents? Why do we wake up remembering the great intentions we had the night before?

Perhaps we are depending upon ourselves rather than on God. The more control we give to God, the more control we have of ourselves. By contrast, the more we depend on ourselves, the more we depend on other things. That's why so many people are dependent on drugs or alcohol. Drugs and alcohol simply take control of one's mind. The "attitude adjustment hour" is well-named because when drinking diminishes willpower, it excludes both God's control and our own self-control. The "happy hour," on the other hand, is not well-named. If we must depend on a drink for our happiness, we are only artificially and temporarily happy.

Imagine—we can be under God's control, have more self-control, and enjoy genuine happiness at the same time!

Self-Control

> Like a city whose walls are broken down
>> is a man who lacks self-control.
>
> Proverbs 25:28

> A fool gives full vent to his anger,
>> but a wise man keeps himself under control.
>
> Proverbs 29:11

Rashness

> It is a trap for a man to dedicate something rashly
>> and only later to consider his vows.
>
> Proverbs 20:25

> The plans of the diligent lead to profit
>> as surely as haste leads to poverty.
>
> Proverbs 21:5

> What you have seen with your eyes
>> do not bring hastily to court,
> for what will you do in the end
>> if your neighbor puts you to shame?
>
> Proverbs 25:8

Do you see a man who speaks in haste?
> There is more hope for a fool than for him.
>> PROVERBS 29:20

Temper and Patience

A fool shows his annoyance at once,
> but a prudent man overlooks an insult.
>> PROVERBS 12:16

A wise man fears the LORD and shuns evil,
> but a fool is hotheaded and reckless.

A quick-tempered man does foolish things,
> and a crafty man is hated.
>> PROVERBS 14:16-17

A patient man has great understanding,
> but a quick-tempered man displays folly.
>> PROVERBS 14:29

A hot-tempered man stirs up dissension,
> but a patient man calms a quarrel.
>> PROVERBS 15:18

Better a patient man than a warrior,
> a man who controls his temper than one who takes
>> a city.
>>> PROVERBS 16:32

A man's wisdom gives him patience;
> it is to his glory to overlook an offense.
>> PROVERBS 19:11

A hot-tempered man must pay the penalty;
> if you rescue him, you will have to do it again.
>> PROVERBS 19:19

Do not make friends with a hot-tempered man,
    do not associate with one easily angered,
or you may learn his ways
    and get yourself ensnared.

Proverbs 22:24-25

Mockers stir up a city,
    but wise men turn away anger.

Proverbs 29:8

An angry man stirs up dissension,
    and a hot-tempered one commits many sins.

Proverbs 29:22

Drunkenness and Gluttony

Wine is a mocker and beer a brawler;
    whoever is led astray by them is not wise.

Proverbs 20:1

Listen, my son, and be wise,
    and keep your heart on the right path.
Do not join those who drink too much wine
    or gorge themselves on meat,
for drunkards and gluttons become poor,
    and drowsiness clothes them in rags.

Proverbs 23:19-21

Who has woe? Who has sorrow?
    Who has strife? Who has complaints?
    Who has needless bruises? Who has bloodshot
        eyes?
Those who linger over wine,
    who go to sample bowls of mixed wine.
Do not gaze at wine when it is red,

when it sparkles in the cup,
    when it goes down smoothly!
In the end it bites like a snake
    and poisons like a viper.
Your eyes will see strange sights
    and your mind imagine confusing things.
You will be like one sleeping on the high seas,
    lying on top of the rigging.
"They hit me," you will say, "but I'm not hurt!
    They beat me, but I don't feel it!
When will I wake up
    so I can find another drink?"

PROVERBS 23:29-35

Psalms

IN THE CASE OF DRUNKENNESS, LOSS OF SELF-CONTROL is self-evident. But what one says and does while stone sober is the real test of self-control. Alcohol may rob a person of good judgment, yet there is an equally great threat from the unbridled tongue. Given the slightest opportunity, one's speech can hijack self-control ever so quickly—surprising even the one who is speaking. Where did those words come from? From whence the embarrassing language, from what source the uncharacteristic temper?

For David, the source of the trouble was no real mystery. A direct line runs from the mouth to the heart. And so David prays that his heart might not be drawn to what is evil. Trying to control the mouth is like shutting the barn door after the horses have already bolted. The only way to ensure self-control in every area of our lives is to go back to the heart of the matter—the heart.

O Lord, I call to you; come quickly to me.
    Hear my voice when I call to you.
May my prayer be set before you like incense;
    may the lifting up of my hands be like the evening
        sacrifice.
Set a guard over my mouth, O Lord;
    keep watch over the door of my lips.
Let not my heart be drawn to what is evil,
    to take part in wicked deeds
with men who are evildoers;
    let me not eat of their delicacies.

Let a righteous man strike me—it is a kindness;
    let him rebuke me—it is oil on my head.
    My head will not refuse it.

Yet my prayer is ever against the deeds of evildoers;
    their rulers will be thrown down from the cliffs,
    and the wicked will learn that my words were well
        spoken.
[They will say,] "As one plows and breaks up the earth,
    so our bones have been scattered at the mouth of
        the grave."

But my eyes are fixed on you, O Sovereign Lord;
    in you I take refuge—do not give me over to death.
Keep me from the snares they have laid for me,
    from the traps set by evildoers.
Let the wicked fall into their own nets,
    while I pass by in safety.

Psalm 141

The Gift of Gracious Speech

How often do you stick your foot into your mouth? When was the last time you spoke before knowing all the facts? Do you recall an instance in which you decided not to say anything, but regrettably, you changed your mind at the last minute? Thinking before we talk is difficult enough; not saying anything at all is next to impossible.

Is this because we overestimate the value of what we have to say? Or because we just can't wait to share our insight with others? At times, of course, what we know can be beneficial to another person, and we are morally obliged to share it. But timing is key, as are our attitude and tone of voice. Solomon has something humorous to say, for example, about a man who loudly blesses his neighbor at an early hour of the morning.

One of the best reasons for remaining silent is that we all have so much to learn from other people. As long as *we* are talking, someone else is not. And if he has a valuable insight to share, we will miss it.

If you are looking for a way to make up for all the times you have spoken out of turn, here it is. Can you remember some kind words someone directed to you lately? How did they make you feel? Each of us takes enough abuse daily to make us appreciate friends who say something cheerful or go out of their way just to say hello. Are we that friend to others? Do we go out of our way to say encouraging things?

Words can also be written. Can you think of someone who would appreciate a friendly note? Everyone welcomes uplifting words.

Wise and Foolish Talk

A fool's talk brings a rod to his back,
     but the lips of the wise protect them.

PROVERBS 14:3

The tongue of the wise commends knowledge,
     but the mouth of the fool gushes folly.

PROVERBS 15:2

The lips of the wise spread knowledge;
     not so the hearts of fools.

PROVERBS 15:7

A wise man's heart guides his mouth,
     and his lips promote instruction.

PROVERBS 16:23

A fool's lips bring him strife,
     and his mouth invites a beating.

A fool's mouth is his undoing,
     and his lips are a snare to his soul.

PROVERBS 18:6-7

Better a poor man whose walk is blameless
    than a fool whose lips are perverse.
PROVERBS 19:1

My son, if your heart is wise,
    then my heart will be glad;
my inmost being will rejoice
    when your lips speak what is right.
PROVERBS 23:15-16

Righteous and Wicked Talk

The tongue of the righteous is choice silver,
    but the heart of the wicked is of little value.

The lips of the righteous nourish many,
    but fools die for lack of judgment.
PROVERBS 10:20-21

The mouth of the righteous brings forth wisdom,
    but a perverse tongue will be cut out.

The lips of the righteous know what is fitting,
    but the mouth of the wicked only what is perverse.
PROVERBS 10:31-32

Through the blessing of the upright a city is exalted,
    but by the mouth of the wicked it is destroyed.
PROVERBS 11:11

An evil man is trapped by his sinful talk,
    but a righteous man escapes trouble.

From the fruit of his lips a man is filled with good
        things
    as surely as the work of his hands rewards him.
PROVERBS 12:13-14

From the fruit of his lips a man enjoys good things,
    but the unfaithful have a craving for violence.

Proverbs 13:2

The heart of the righteous weighs its answers,
    but the mouth of the wicked gushes evil.

Proverbs 15:28

A wicked man listens to evil lips;
    a liar pays attention to a malicious tongue.

Proverbs 17:4

Appropriate Speech

A man finds joy in giving an apt reply—
    and how good is a timely word!

Proverbs 15:23

The wise in heart are called discerning,
    and pleasant words promote instruction.

Proverbs 16:21

Pleasant words are a honeycomb,
    sweet to the soul and healing to the bones.

Proverbs 16:24

A word aptly spoken
    is like apples of gold in settings of silver.

Proverbs 25:11

If a man loudly blesses his neighbor early in the
            morning,
    it will be taken as a curse.

Proverbs 27:14

Maintaining Silence

When words are many, sin is not absent,
but he who holds his tongue is wise.

PROVERBS 10:19

A prudent man keeps his knowledge to himself,
but the heart of fools blurts out folly.

PROVERBS 12:23

He who guards his lips guards his life,
but he who speaks rashly will come to ruin.

PROVERBS 13:3

Even a fool is thought wise if he keeps silent,
and discerning if he holds his tongue.

PROVERBS 17:28

He who answers before listening—
that is his folly and his shame.

PROVERBS 18:13

He who guards his mouth and his tongue
keeps himself from calamity.

PROVERBS 21:23

Controlled Speech

A gentle answer turns away wrath,
but a harsh word stirs up anger.

PROVERBS 15:1

A man of knowledge uses words with restraint,
and a man of understanding is even-tempered.

PROVERBS 17:27

Through patience a ruler can be persuaded,
and a gentle tongue can break a bone.

PROVERBS 25:15

Psalms

To be or not to be?" is not the question that David asks
in the psalm that follows. For David, the question is, "To
speak or not to speak?" Everything within him wants to
shout out to God about the cruel brevity of his life. But in
an act of extraordinary self-control, David remains silent,
for evil men in his presence were bound to relish any challenge he might make to God.

The person of discernment knows when to speak and
when to refrain. How does he know? He considers his
perspective, consciously discerning factors such as the
right time and the right place. When you think of it, that
is David's very concern. To know the brevity of one's life
is to gain a perspective that wisely prioritizes one's life,
one's time, one's money—and even one's words.

I said, "I will watch my ways
and keep my tongue from sin;
I will put a muzzle on my mouth
as long as the wicked are in my presence."
But when I was silent and still,
not even saying anything good,
my anguish increased.
My heart grew hot within me,
and as I meditated, the fire burned;
then I spoke with my tongue:

"Show me, O LORD, my life's end
and the number of my days;

let me know how fleeting is my life.
You have made my days a mere handbreadth;
 the span of my years is as nothing before you.
 Each man's life is but a breath.   *Selah*
Man is a mere phantom as he goes to and fro:
 He bustles about, but only in vain;
 he heaps up wealth, not knowing who will get it.

"But now, Lord, what do I look for?
 My hope is in you.
Save me from all my transgressions;
 do not make me the scorn of fools.
I was silent; I would not open my mouth,
 for you are the one who has done this.
Remove your scourge from me;
 I am overcome by the blow of your hand.
You rebuke and discipline men for their sin;
 you consume their wealth like a moth—
 each man is but a breath.

            Selah

"Hear my prayer, O LORD,
 listen to my cry for help;
 be not deaf to my weeping.
For I dwell with you as an alien,
 a stranger, as all my fathers were.
Look away from me, that I may rejoice again
 before I depart and am no more."

PSALM 39

When Talk Turns Malicious

HAVE YOU EVER PLAYED THE GAME GOSSIP? The first player whispers something to the second player, who repeats it quickly to a third, and so on around the room. When the last player has received the message, he tells the group what the first player supposedly said. Then the first player tells what he actually said. Invariably, everyone laughs because what the first player said and what the last player heard are vastly different.

Gossip can be fun when it is played as a game. When played in real life, it is incredibly destructive. Wisdom teaches that what we say has the power of life and death. Words can pierce a person's soul, either for good or for ill. But gossip can hurt us even if we ourselves never hear the words. It can damage one of our most precious assets—our reputation—behind our back without offering any opportunity for explanation or clarification. If we were in a court of law, such hearsay talk would not be admissible. It is untrustworthy and unreliable.

Even if what one repeats is the truth, a breach of trust is almost always involved. Gossip is not worth repeating unless it is "juicy," so the information has usually been revealed only in confidence. People need to know that they can share things that are personally troubling or embarrassing without risk that the whole world will know.

Part of the problem with gossip is the attitude of those willing to listen to it. When they are willing to believe the worst about a person, based on second- or thirdhand information, they become accomplices in the gossip's guilt.

When real-life gossip becomes so much like the game that the original message is distorted, false information is perpetuated. At that point the person who gossips is spreading lies. Solomon says that God hates lips that lie. Lying lips, slandering lips, and lips that love to gossip are lips that destroy. What kind of lips do we have?

Flattery

> A lying tongue hates those it hurts,
>   and a flattering mouth works ruin.
>
> PROVERBS 26:28

> He who rebukes a man will in the end gain more favor
>   than he who has a flattering tongue.
>
> PROVERBS 28:23

> Whoever flatters his neighbor
>   is spreading a net for his feet.
>
> PROVERBS 29:5

Slander and Gossip

> He who conceals his hatred has lying lips,
>   and whoever spreads slander is a fool.
>
> PROVERBS 10:18

A gossip betrays a confidence,
>but a trustworthy man keeps a secret.

PROVERBS 11:13

A perverse man stirs up dissension,
>and a gossip separates close friends.

PROVERBS 16:28

He who covers over an offense promotes love,
>but whoever repeats the matter separates close
>>friends.

PROVERBS 17:9

The words of a gossip are like choice morsels;
>they go down to a man's inmost parts.

PROVERBS 18:8; 26:22

A gossip betrays a confidence;
>so avoid a man who talks too much.

PROVERBS 20:19

Without wood a fire goes out;
>without gossip a quarrel dies down.

PROVERBS 26:20

Hurtful Talk

A man who lacks judgment derides his neighbor,
>but a man of understanding holds his tongue.

PROVERBS 11:12

Reckless words pierce like a sword,
>but the tongue of the wise brings healing.

PROVERBS 12:18

The tongue that brings healing is a tree of life,
    but a deceitful tongue crushes the spirit.

PROVERBS 15:4

A scoundrel plots evil,
    and his speech is like a scorching fire.

PROVERBS 16:27

As a north wind brings rain,
    so a sly tongue brings angry looks.

PROVERBS 25:23

Like a fluttering sparrow or a darting swallow,
    an undeserved curse does not come to rest.

PROVERBS 26:2

Quarreling

Starting a quarrel is like breaching a dam;
    so drop the matter before a dispute breaks out.

PROVERBS 17:14

He who loves a quarrel loves sin;
    he who builds a high gate invites destruction.

PROVERBS 17:19

It is to a man's honor to avoid strife,
    but every fool is quick to quarrel.

PROVERBS 20:3

Drive out the mocker, and out goes strife;
    quarrels and insults are ended.

PROVERBS 22:10

As charcoal to embers and as wood to fire,
    so is a quarrelsome man for kindling strife.

PROVERBS 26:21

Lying

Truthful lips endure forever,
> but a lying tongue lasts only a moment.

PROVERBS 12:19

The LORD detests lying lips,
> but he delights in men who are truthful.

PROVERBS 12:22

A man of perverse heart does not prosper;
> he whose tongue is deceitful falls into trouble.

PROVERBS 17:20

A false witness will not go unpunished,
> and he who pours out lies will not go free.

PROVERBS 19:5

What a man desires is unfailing love;
> better to be poor than a liar.

PROVERBS 19:22

A fortune made by a lying tongue
> is a fleeting vapor and a deadly snare.

PROVERBS 21:6

The Power of the Tongue

From the fruit of his mouth a man's stomach is filled;
> with the harvest from his lips he is satisfied.

The tongue has the power of life and death,
> and those who love it will eat its fruit.

PROVERBS 18:20-21

Psalms

THE UNKINDEST CUT OF ALL" MAY NOT BE FROM a dagger but from the slander that cuts a good man down before his time. Anyone who has ever been on the receiving end of lies and slander will readily identify with the pain and anguish that David must have experienced. At least flattery is a deception told to your face. You, yourself, can decide how to respond. By contrast, the accusing tongue behind your back is virtually unstoppable. What, if anything, can be done about it? As long as some people are willing to distort the truth and other people are eager to believe the worst, slander can be assured of a long life.

Yet we can all take comfort from knowing that we're not the first to experience the abusive power of the tongue. Twisting Jesus' words beyond all recognition, our Lord's accusers spoke the most malicious lies ever perpetrated. So if slander comes our way, at least we're in good company.

Be merciful to me, O Lord, for I am in distress;
    my eyes grow weak with sorrow,
    my soul and my body with grief.
My life is consumed by anguish
    and my years by groaning;
my strength fails because of my affliction,
    and my bones grow weak.
Because of all my enemies,
    I am the utter contempt of my neighbors;
I am a dread to my friends—
    those who see me on the street flee from me.
I am forgotten by them as though I were dead;
    I have become like broken pottery.

When Talk Turns Malicious

For I hear the slander of many;
    there is terror on every side;
they conspire against me
    and plot to take my life.

But I trust in you, O LORD;
    I say, "You are my God."
My times are in your hands;
    deliver me from my enemies
    and from those who pursue me.
Let your face shine on your servant;
    save me in your unfailing love.
Let me not be put to shame, O LORD,
    for I have cried out to you;
but let the wicked be put to shame
    and lie silent in the grave.
Let their lying lips be silenced,
    for with pride and contempt
    they speak arrogantly against the righteous.

How great is your goodness,
    which you have stored up for those who fear you,
which you bestow in the sight of men
    on those who take refuge in you.
In the shelter of your presence you hide them
    from the intrigues of men;
in your dwelling you keep them safe
    from accusing tongues.

PSALM 31:9-20

Stirring Up Trouble

Do you feel safe living in your neighborhood? Has anyone you know been the victim of a brutal attack? Do you think our society is increasingly violent? Will wars and fighting ever end? We live in a world of conflict, much of it physical conflict. As if the streets did not have enough violence, we bring it into the football stadium and hockey arena or into our homes by television.

Violence is deplorable. Few people will argue with that. Our generation has no monopoly on violence. American history is filled with war and frontier justice. Not many of us are physically violent, although substantial domestic violence toward spouses and children can even be found in some "good" homes. But dissension and conflict can exist without physical violence.

Solomon suggests that we stir up conflict when we conspire with our coworkers at the office and spend our time in political maneuvering. When we insist on revenge, we escalate conflict that someone else started. This creates a vicious circle, and we get ourselves needlessly into trouble. Considering the trouble each of us already has, why do we ask for more? Sometimes we let other people talk us into being part of the problem. Hardly anyone headed for trouble wants to go alone; troublemakers insist that we go along with them.

Violent and nonviolent conflict are clearly related. An act of violence can be prevented if the nonviolent conflict preceding it is avoided. We say we are not violent people, but might our conduct lead someone else in that direction? On the positive side, what have we done to encourage harmony within our family? What have we contributed to the safety of our citizens or to peace among the nations?

Solicitation to Evil

My son, if sinners entice you,
    do not give in to them.
If they say, "Come along with us;
    let's lie in wait for someone's blood,
    let's waylay some harmless soul;
let's swallow them alive, like the grave,
    and whole, like those who go down to the pit;
we will get all sorts of valuable things
    and fill our houses with plunder;
throw in your lot with us,
    and we will share a common purse"—
my son, do not go along with them,
    do not set foot on their paths;
for their feet rush into sin,
    they are swift to shed blood.
How useless to spread a net
    in full view of all the birds!
These men lie in wait for their own blood;
    they waylay only themselves!
Such is the end of all who go after ill-gotten gain;
    it takes away the lives of those who get it.

PROVERBS 1:10-19

A violent man entices his neighbor
    and leads him down a path that is not good.

PROVERBS 16:29

Like a muddied spring or a polluted well
>is a righteous man who gives way to the wicked.
PROVERBS 25:26

Stone is heavy and sand a burden,
>but provocation by a fool is heavier than both.
PROVERBS 27:3

He who leads the upright along an evil path
>will fall into his own trap,
>but the blameless will receive a good inheritance.
PROVERBS 28:10

Violence

Do not envy a violent man
>or choose any of his ways,
for the LORD detests a perverse man
>but takes the upright into his confidence.
PROVERBS 3:31-32

The violence of the wicked will drag them away,
>for they refuse to do what is right.
PROVERBS 21:7

A wicked man puts up a bold front,
>but an upright man gives thought to his ways.
PROVERBS 21:29

Murderers

A man tormented by the guilt of murder
>will be a fugitive till death;
>let no one support him.

PROVERBS 28:17

Causing Others Harm

Do not plot harm against your neighbor,
    who lives trustfully near you.
Do not accuse a man for no reason—
    when he has done you no harm.

Proverbs 3:29-30

Revenge

Do not say, "I'll pay you back for this wrong!"
    Wait for the Lord, and he will deliver you.

Proverbs 20:22

Do not testify against your neighbor without cause,
    or use your lips to deceive.
Do not say, "I'll do to him as he has done to me;
    I'll pay that man back for what he did."

Proverbs 24:28-29

Dissension and Strife

There are six things the Lord hates,
    seven that are detestable to him:
        haughty eyes,
        a lying tongue,
        hands that shed innocent blood,
        a heart that devises wicked schemes,
        feet that are quick to rush into evil,
        a false witness who pours out lies
        and a man who stirs up dissension among
            brothers.

Proverbs 6:16-19

Better a dry crust with peace and quiet
    than a house full of feasting, with strife.

Proverbs 17:1

Casting the lot settles disputes
 and keeps strong opponents apart.

PROVERBS 18:18

An offended brother is more unyielding than a
 fortified city,
 and disputes are like the barred gates of a citadel.

PROVERBS 18:19

Meddling

Like one who seizes a dog by the ears
 is a passer-by who meddles in a quarrel not his
 own.

PROVERBS 26:17

Psalms

IT WOULD BE ALL TOO EASY TO DISMISS THIS SECTION of collected proverbs as applying only to the mafia or conspiratorial terrorists. But David is just about to tell us of another group of terrorists: the verbal mafia—those who sit around sharpening their tongues and destroying folks with what they say about them. Would you be surprised to learn that murderous conspirators like this are frequently found within churches? Even the Lord's body has conspiring cliques, slander campaigns, and plots to overthrow. You'll also find all of this on the campuses of Christian colleges and universities, where conspiratorial infighting can be all the more intense because the stakes are so low.

But, at the mere mention of how Christians in the church can be the worst offenders, maybe I've quit preaching and (contrary to that last proverb) gone to meddling!

Hear me, O God, as I voice my complaint;
    protect my life from the threat of the enemy.
Hide me from the conspiracy of the wicked,
    from that noisy crowd of evildoers.

They sharpen their tongues like swords
    and aim their words like deadly arrows.
They shoot from ambush at the innocent man;
    they shoot at him suddenly, without fear.

They encourage each other in evil plans,
    they talk about hiding their snares;
    they say, "Who will see them?"
They plot injustice and say,
    "We have devised a perfect plan!"
    Surely the mind and heart of man are cunning.

But God will shoot them with arrows;
    suddenly they will be struck down.
He will turn their own tongues against them
    and bring them to ruin;
    all who see them will shake their heads in scorn.

All mankind will fear;
    they will proclaim the works of God
    and ponder what he has done.
Let the righteous rejoice in the LORD
    and take refuge in him;
    let all the upright in heart praise him!

PSALM 64

Old-Fashioned Honesty

How do you define the word *honesty*? As truthfulness? As freedom from deception? As accuracy? As integrity? As legitimacy? When Proverbs refers to honesty, all of those definitions are included. Proverbs calls for truthful answers, social interaction without deception, accurate weights and measures, integrity in business transactions, and legitimate profits. Common to all those aspects of honesty is the idea of trust, which is at the heart of every relationship, whether personal or social. If trust is the glue that holds us together, dishonesty is the force that will tear us apart. Honesty is not just the best policy; it is a moral mandate to assure the viability of other moral concerns.

Is your definition of honesty somewhat different? Many people use the word to mean something radically different—for example, openness, unashamed revealing of one's darker side, or freedom to say what is on one's mind even if it may hurt somebody. A book or movie focusing on a clandestine love affair is touted as being "stunningly honest" or filled with "courage and candor." Some people feel tremendous relief when they "come out of the closet" because now they can be "honest" about themselves without moral incrimination. Almost nothing is considered a sin today as long as you are "honest" about who you are and what you do. In fact, the only unforgivable sin today is the sin of not being honest, as honesty has been redefined.

Hypocrisy is no virtue, and failure to fully disclose can be a vice. But the "new honesty" is far from acceptable in Wisdom's eyes. It has become a mask for immoral behavior that violates our commitment to God's Word, which true honesty would require us to obey. The "new honesty" is itself deceptive and illegitimate. It does not accurately measure God's will, and it renounces moral integrity.

If we are supposed to "tell it like it is," then we have to be honest: The "new honesty" is a moral sham. The old honesty is still honorable.

Proverbs

Truthfulness

There is deceit in the hearts of those who plot evil,
> but joy for those who promote peace.

PROVERBS 12:20

The righteous hate what is false,
> but the wicked bring shame and disgrace.

PROVERBS 13:5

An honest answer
> is like a kiss on the lips.

PROVERBS 24:26

Like a madman shooting
> firebrands or deadly arrows
is a man who deceives his neighbor
> and says, "I was only joking!"

PROVERBS 26:18-19

Accurate Weights

The LORD abhors dishonest scales,
 but accurate weights are his delight.

PROVERBS 11:1

Honest scales and balances are from the LORD:
 all the weights in the bag are of his making.

PROVERBS 16:11

Differing weights and differing measures—
 the LORD detests them both.

PROVERBS 20:10

The LORD detests differing weights,
 and dishonest scales do not please him.

PROVERBS 20:23

Boundary Stones

Do not move an ancient boundary stone
 set up by your forefathers.

PROVERBS 22:28

Do not move an ancient boundary stone
 or encroach on the fields of the fatherless,
for their Defender is strong;
 he will take up their case against you.

PROVERBS 23:10-11

Wrongfully Obtained Gains

Ill-gotten treasures are of no value,
 but righteousness delivers from death.

PROVERBS 10:2

Dishonest money dwindles away,
> but he who gathers money little by little makes it
> grow.

PROVERBS 13:11

Food gained by fraud tastes sweet to a man,
> but he ends up with a mouth full of gravel.

PROVERBS 20:17

An inheritance quickly gained at the beginning
> will not be blessed at the end.

PROVERBS 20:21

Bribery

A greedy man brings trouble to his family,
> but he who hates bribes will live.

PROVERBS 15:27

A bribe is a charm to the one who gives it;
> wherever he turns, he succeeds.

PROVERBS 17:8

A wicked man accepts a bribe in secret
> to pervert the course of justice.

PROVERBS 17:23

A gift given in secret soothes anger,
> and a bribe concealed in the cloak pacifies great
> wrath.

PROVERBS 21:14

Psalms

DON'T YOU LOVE THE WAY GOD USES IRONY? Having been warned by Proverbs not to deal in extortion and theft, we see in the psalm that follows an allusion to how God will weigh in the balance all those who insist on dealing dishonestly in business or personal relationships. Weighed on divine scales, evildoers will not be able to complain of unfair business practices like their own. God's scales of justice are always correct, never tilted by greed or favoritism.

If dishonesty with scales and balances seems a bit arcane in our modern world, try thinking in terms of corporate and consumer fraud, accounting scandals, and so-called white-collar crime. Regardless of how sophisticated society becomes, the day is coming when some old-fashioned scales will still weigh the guilty in the balance.

My soul finds rest in God alone;
    my salvation comes from him.
He alone is my rock and my salvation;
    he is my fortress, I will never be shaken.

How long will you assault a man?
    Would all of you throw him down—
    this leaning wall, this tottering fence?
They fully intend to topple him
    from his lofty place;
    they take delight in lies.
With their mouths they bless,
    but in their hearts they curse.

Selah

Find rest, O my soul, in God alone;
    my hope comes from him.
He alone is my rock and my salvation;
    he is my fortress, I will not be shaken.
My salvation and my honor depend on God;
    he is my mighty rock, my refuge.
Trust in him at all times, O people;
    pour out your hearts to him,
    for God is our refuge.

Selah

Lowborn men are but a breath,
    the highborn are but a lie;
if weighed on a balance, they are nothing;
    together they are only a breath.
Do not trust in extortion
    or take pride in stolen goods;
though your riches increase,
    do not set your heart on them.

One thing God has spoken,
    two things have I heard:
that you, O God, are strong,
    and that you, O Lord, are loving.
Surely you will reward each person
    according to what he has done.

PSALM 62

In Search of Justice

WHAT DO YOU THINK OF OUR JUDICIAL SYSTEM? Does it work? Are we really a nation of justice? For all? Equally? Do criminals get what is coming to them? Are victims vindicated? Is the system too harsh or too lenient? Are our civil rights sufficiently protected?

God calls us to justice, to fairness, to giving due respect. As our Creator, He has endowed us with rights that no governing power can give us and that no governing power should take away. In the commandments that He handed down through Moses, God gave honor to law and to its important role in society. When a person is accused of a crime, God calls for a careful balance so that no innocent person is convicted and no guilty person is set free.

God's prophets preached social justice for the poor and politically oppressed. In the wilderness, John the Baptist linked together religious observance and practical justice. Jesus taught His disciples to care about those in prisons, apparently including even those who belonged there. From cover to cover, the Bible is a book of justice.

Why such attention to justice? Because we are all being judged. Each day people scrutinize and judge our actions. We too make judgments about other people. Is our judging fair? Do we unfairly accuse? Do we favor others with a presumption of innocence? Do we demand sufficient proof before condemnation? Do we show mercy from our lofty judge's bench? Do we exonerate those who trespass against us? Do we extend a helping hand to the hungry and homeless? Do we hear the cry of the lonely? Which of their rights have we failed to consider?

The temple of justice has many levels. At the top of the temple is a courtroom made for eternity. Justice there is not blind. In that court the Judge knows all. He is Himself the truthful witness. He will neither condemn the innocent nor acquit the guilty. In that court all wrongs will be made right and every good will find its reward. No more will justice be delayed or denied, and mercy will flow like a river.

We should question just how well our judicial system is working. And we must continue to seek justice in our land. But even more important, we must ask ourselves, How do we individually respond as ministers of justice?

False Witnesses

> A truthful witness gives honest testimony,
>> but a false witness tells lies.

PROVERBS 12:17

> A truthful witness does not deceive,
>> but a false witness pours out lies.

PROVERBS 14:5

> A truthful witness saves lives,
>> but a false witness is deceitful.

PROVERBS 14:25

A false witness will not go unpunished,
    and he who pours out lies will perish.

Proverbs 19:9

A corrupt witness mocks at justice,
    and the mouth of the wicked gulps down evil.

Proverbs 19:28

A false witness will perish,
    and whoever listens to him will be destroyed
        forever.

Proverbs 21:28

Like a club or a sword or a sharp arrow
    is the man who gives false testimony against his
        neighbor.

Proverbs 25:18

Open-Mindedness

The first to present his case seems right,
    till another comes forward and questions him.

Proverbs 18:17

Judicial Justice

Acquitting the guilty and condemning the innocent—
    the Lord detests them both.

Proverbs 17:15

It is not good to punish an innocent man,
    or to flog officials for their integrity.

Proverbs 17:26

It is not good to be partial to the wicked
    or to deprive the innocent of justice.

Proverbs 18:5

When justice is done, it brings joy to the righteous
    but terror to evildoers.

PROVERBS 21:15

Rescue those being led away to death;
    hold back those staggering toward slaughter.
If you say, "But we know nothing about this,"
    does not he who weighs the heart perceive it?
Does not he who guards your life know it?
    Will he not repay each person according to what
        he has done?

PROVERBS 24:11-12

To show partiality in judging is not good:
Whoever says to the guilty, "You are innocent"—
    peoples will curse him and nations denounce him.
But it will go well with those who convict the guilty,
    and rich blessing will come upon them.

PROVERBS 24:23-25

Evil men do not understand justice,
    but those who seek the LORD understand it fully.

PROVERBS 28:5

Many seek an audience with a ruler,
    but it is from the LORD that man gets justice.

PROVERBS 29:26

Psalms

DO YOU THINK THAT "CHRISTIAN LAWYER" OR "Christian
politician" are oxymorons, like "deafening silence" or
"sweet sorrow"? Who more than lawyers, judges, legisla-
tors, and governors ought to have a high view of justice

that is drawn from Christ's own teaching? Both within and without the halls of government, we need men and women of principle who will convict the guilty and defend those who are falsely accused, who will come to the aid of an often-tyrannized underclass, and who will champion the fair treatment of all people.

In God's government, God Himself is our wise and merciful Judge, Christ is our advocate before the Father, and God's perfect law never turns a blind eye to injustice. Can we match that high view of justice in our own personal relations with others?

> Do you rulers indeed speak justly?
>> Do you judge uprightly among men?
> No, in your heart you devise injustice,
>> and your hands mete out violence on the earth.
> Even from birth the wicked go astray;
>> from the womb they are wayward and speak lies.
> Their venom is like the venom of a snake,
>> like that of a cobra that has stopped its ears,
> that will not heed the tune of the charmer,
>> however skillful the enchanter may be.
>
> Break the teeth in their mouths, O God;
>> tear out, O Lord, the fangs of the lions!
> Let them vanish like water that flows away;
>> when they draw the bow, let their arrows be
>>> blunted.
> Like a slug melting away as it moves along,
>> like a stillborn child, may they not see the sun.
>
> Before your pots can feel [the heat of] the thorns—
>> whether they be green or dry—the wicked will be
>>> swept away.

The righteous will be glad when they are avenged,
> when they bathe their feet in the blood of the
> > wicked.

Then men will say,
> "Surely the righteous still are rewarded;
> surely there is a God who judges the earth."

Psalm 58

Money: A Trivial Pursuit

Do you think it ironic that the words "In God We Trust" are found on currency? We need to be reminded where to put our trust, and our currency is a perfect place for that reminder. If God has a competitor for our trust, surely it is money—or the things that money can buy.

Of course, everyone knows that money cannot buy some things. Why then do we keep hoping it can? Why do we insist on working overtime to buy more happiness, sometimes while marriages and families are falling apart? Why do we feel so insecure when the stock market drops a percentage point? Why do we lose sleep when interest rates change, or worry about the housing market?

God promises to give us all we need and warns us that wealth may not even be in our best interest. Often our love of money gets us into more trouble than we could ever imagine. In fact, money's questionable reputation is so well-known that many nonbiblical proverbs advise against too strong an attachment to it. Like Solomon's own proverbs, these remind us that money is here today and gone tomorrow—that we can't take it with us.

The problem with material possessions is that they divert attention from our true spiritual nature. They focus on the material world, which is only temporary. When we concentrate on creature comforts, we lose sight of the greater life to come, where we will not go bankrupt and our blessings cannot be stolen in the night.

Wealth and Poverty

Honor the LORD with your wealth,
    with the firstfruits of all your crops;
then your barns will be filled to overflowing,
    and your vats will brim over with new wine.

PROVERBS 3:9-10

The wealth of the rich is their fortified city,
    but poverty is the ruin of the poor.

PROVERBS 10:15

Wealth is worthless in the day of wrath,
    but righteousness delivers from death.

PROVERBS 11:4

Whoever trusts in his riches will fall,
    but the righteous will thrive like a green leaf.

PROVERBS 11:28

A man's riches may ransom his life,
    but a poor man hears no threat.

PROVERBS 13:8

The poor are shunned even by their neighbors,
    but the rich have many friends.

PROVERBS 14:20

Better a little with the fear of the LORD
than great wealth with turmoil.

PROVERBS 15:16

Of what use is money in the hand of a fool,
since he has no desire to get wisdom?

PROVERBS 17:16

The wealth of the rich is their fortified city;
they imagine it an unscalable wall.

PROVERBS 18:11

A poor man pleas for mercy,
but a rich man answers harshly.

PROVERBS 18:23

Wealth brings many friends,
but a poor man's friend deserts him.

PROVERBS 19:4

Many curry favor with a ruler,
and everyone is the friend of a man who gives
gifts.

A poor man is shunned by all his relatives—
how much more do his friends avoid him!
Though he pursues them with pleading,
they are nowhere to be found.

PROVERBS 19:6-7

Rich and poor have this in common:
The LORD is the Maker of them all.

PROVERBS 22:2

The rich rule over the poor,
  and the borrower is servant to the lender.

Proverbs 22:7

Do not wear yourself out to get rich;
  have the wisdom to show restraint.
Cast but a glance at riches, and they are gone,
  for they will surely sprout wings
  and fly off to the sky like an eagle.

Proverbs 23:4-5

He who is full loathes honey,
  but to the hungry even what is bitter tastes sweet.

Proverbs 27:7

Better a poor man whose walk is blameless
  than a rich man whose ways are perverse.

Proverbs 28:6

He who increases his wealth by exorbitant interest
  amasses it for another, who will be kind to the
    poor.

Proverbs 28:8

A rich man may be wise in his own eyes,
  but a poor man who has discernment sees through
    him.

Proverbs 28:11

A faithful man will be richly blessed,
  but one eager to get rich will not go unpunished.

To show partiality is not good—
  yet a man will do wrong for a piece of bread.

A stingy man is eager to get rich
and is unaware that poverty awaits him.

PROVERBS 28:20-22

Psalms

IN THE WORLD OF HIGH FINANCE AND ACCOUNTING, the
bottom line tells the final story of profit or loss. Interesting,
isn't it, that when both the proverbs of Solomon and the
psalms of David speak about the relative value of material
wealth, invariably we are brought to the real bottom line,
which is death? The loss incurred at that point reminds us
of the story of the wealthy widow about whom someone
asked: "How much did she leave?" From the back of the
room came the insightful answer: "Everything."

The profits appearing on our bottom line at the point of
death are determined by the investments we have made in
this life. Are our personal portfolios spiritual or carnal?
And what was the rate of interest in the salvation of our
souls?

Hear this, all you peoples;
listen, all who live in this world,
both low and high,
rich and poor alike:
My mouth will speak words of wisdom;
the utterance from my heart will give
understanding.
I will turn my ear to a proverb;
with the harp I will expound my riddle:

Why should I fear when evil days come,
when wicked deceivers surround me—

those who trust in their wealth
 and boast of their great riches?
No man can redeem the life of another
 or give to God a ransom for him—
the ransom for a life is costly,
 no payment is ever enough—
that he should live on forever
 and not see decay.

For all can see that wise men die;
 the foolish and the senseless alike perish
 and leave their wealth to others.
Their tombs will remain their houses forever,
 their dwellings for endless generations,
 though they had named lands after themselves.

But man, despite his riches, does not endure;
 he is like the beasts that perish.

This is the fate of those who trust in themselves,
 and of their followers, who approve their sayings.

Selah

Like sheep they are destined for the grave,
 and death will feed on them.
The upright will rule over them in the morning;
 their forms will decay in the grave,
 far from their princely mansions.
But God will redeem my life from the grave;
 he will surely take me to himself.

Selah

Do not be overawed when a man grows rich,
 when the splendor of his house increases;

for he will take nothing with him when he dies,
    his splendor will not descend with him.
Though while he lived he counted himself blessed—
    and men praise you when you prosper—
he will join the generation of his fathers,
    who will never see the light [of life].

A man who has riches without understanding
    is like the beasts that perish.

PSALM 49

The Challenge of Sharing

Do you wince each time you see pictures of starving children? Do you feel torn between wanting to do something about the problem and wanting to forget their faces, as if they never existed? How do you deal with the abundant blessings you have? Are we supposed to feel guilty for having so much when others have so little? How can we, as seemingly powerless individuals, solve the hunger problems of the world?

When Jesus observed that the world would always have poor people, He did not invite complacency about their condition. Jesus encouraged His disciples to supply the needs of those who are economically deprived and politically oppressed. Solomon sheds light on the enormity of the problem and the limitations we often feel when contributing to the solution. He tells us that we should do good works when we can, when we see the need among those with whom we live—our family, our neighbors, and even strangers who come our way. If we all did our part by sharing with those closest to us, we could easily solve the problem of poverty.

The principle is sound, but many won't or can't do their part. Therefore we are called to seek out and share even with those who may be far away or in a different part of our own city. We must do what we can as citizens to ensure that the little person is not further abused by government policy, that he is not robbed of incentive and pride by being forced to accept handouts, that opportunities exist for him to change his circumstances in life, and that assistance is available while he is making that effort.

Of course, giving brings real joy. We all know that warm feeling when we share what we have with less fortunate people. Most of us are eager to meet any needs that come to our immediate attention. In such an abundant society, however, the challenge is to look beyond our own neighborhood or church to see the needs of other people. The needy may be distasteful to us or foreign to our culture. Solomon says we all have something in common— our Maker. Sharing affirms that we believe this truth.

Proverbs

Benevolence and Generosity

Do not withhold good from those who deserve it,
    when it is in your power to act.
Do not say to your neighbor,
    "Come back later; I'll give it tomorrow"—
    when you now have it with you.

Proverbs 3:27-28

One man gives freely, yet gains even more;
    another withholds unduly, but comes to poverty.

A generous man will prosper;
    he who refreshes others will himself be refreshed.

People curse the man who hoards grain,
    but blessing crowns him who is willing to sell.

Proverbs 11:24-26

A good man leaves an inheritance for his children's
children,
> but a sinner's wealth is stored up for the righteous.
>> PROVERBS 13:22

He who despises his neighbor sins,
> but blessed is he who is kind to the needy.
>> PROVERBS 14:21

A gift opens the way for the giver
> and ushers him into the presence of the great.
>> PROVERBS 18:16

He who is kind to the poor lends to the LORD,
> and he will reward him for what he has done.
>> PROVERBS 19:17

If a man shuts his ears to the cry of the poor,
> he too will cry out and not be answered.
>> PROVERBS 21:13

A generous man will himself be blessed,
> for he shares his food with the poor.
>> PROVERBS 22:9

Like clouds and wind without rain
> is a man who boasts of gifts he does not give.
>> PROVERBS 25:14

He who gives to the poor will lack nothing,
> but he who closes his eyes to them
>> receives many curses.
>>> PROVERBS 28:27

Oppression of the Poor

A poor man's field may produce abundant food,
  but injustice sweeps it away.

Proverbs 13:23

He who oppresses the poor shows contempt for their
    Maker,
  but whoever is kind to the needy honors God.

Proverbs 14:31

All the days of the oppressed are wretched,
  but the cheerful heart has a continual feast.

Proverbs 15:15

Better a little with righteousness
  than much gain with injustice.

Proverbs 16:8

He who oppresses the poor to increase his wealth
  and he who gives gifts to the rich—both
    come to poverty.

Proverbs 22:16

Do not exploit the poor because they are poor
  and do not crush the needy in court,
for the Lord will take up their case
  and will plunder those who plunder them.

Proverbs 22:22-23

The righteous care about justice for the poor,
  but the wicked have no such concern.

Proverbs 29:7

The poor man and the oppressor have this in common:
  The Lord gives sight to the eyes of both.

Proverbs 29:13

Psalms

HAVE YOU NOTICED THAT PROVERBS OF ALL TYPES often seem to be mutually contradictory? What are we supposed to do, for example, when we are cautioned, "Look before you leap," and then we are immediately reminded that "He who hesitates is lost"? More to the point, if we have given sacrificially to meet the needs of the poor, as many proverbs suggest we do, how will we ever have enough left over to be that "good man" who "leaves an inheritance to his children's children"? One must be ever so wise in applying the wisdom of Proverbs.

In that light, what are we to make of this psalm of David in which he decries the man who has hounded to death the poor but then asks God to punish that evil man by having creditors confiscate all his assets and causing the man's children to become wandering beggars? Is this the same David who was a man after God's own heart? Can we give him the benefit of the doubt as we do Jesus when He used brute force to drive the moneychangers out of the temple? Taking a quick reality check in the mirror, just how passionate are we against those (perhaps including ourselves) who give so little thought to people in dire need?

> O God, whom I praise,
>   do not remain silent,
> for wicked and deceitful men
>   have opened their mouths against me;
>   they have spoken against me with lying tongues.
> With words of hatred they surround me;
>   they attack me without cause.
> In return for my friendship they accuse me,

but I am a man of prayer.
They repay me evil for good,
    and hatred for my friendship.
Appoint an evil man to oppose him;
    let an accuser stand at his right hand.
When he is tried, let him be found guilty,
    and may his prayers condemn him.
May his days be few;
    may another take his place of leadership.
May his children be fatherless
    and his wife a widow.
May his children be wandering beggars;
    may they be driven from their ruined homes.
May a creditor seize all he has;
    may strangers plunder the fruits of his labor.
May no one extend kindness to him
    or take pity on his fatherless children.
May his descendants be cut off,
    their names blotted out from the next generation.
May the iniquity of his fathers be remembered before
        the LORD;
    may the sin of his mother never be blotted out.
May their sins always remain before the LORD,
    that he may cut off the memory of them from the
        earth.

For he never thought of doing a kindness,
    but hounded to death the poor
    and the needy and the brokenhearted.

PSALM 109:1-16

Commonsense
Economics

ARE YOU A SELF-STARTER? DO YOU FIND ENJOYMENT in your work? Does the clock move too slowly toward the end of the workday, or are you surprised when the whistle blows and everyone else is heading home? Given a choice, would you sleep until 10:00 A.M., or are you up at the crack of dawn? How would you describe yourself—hardworking, lazy, or one who puts in your day but no more?

Can we choose which type of worker we will be? If we don't mind being poor, is laziness acceptable? If we want to be rich, can we work night and day? On the side of hard work, the so-called Protestant work ethic has been much abused. Too many workaholics have ignored serious family responsibilities. On the other hand, some have abandoned their role as contributors to society. The apostle Paul says of this group, if they won't work, don't feed them.

From Solomon's perspective, laziness is more common than overwork. Wisdom does know us well! Wisdom also knows that we sometimes manage our money unwisely. We are not born thrifty, nor are we always cautious. In curious contrast with the encouragement to supply other people's needs, Proverbs takes a strong position against cosigning a loan. Could it be that Wisdom knows something we don't about someone whose credit is so bad that a cosigner is necessary? Are we really doing someone a favor by letting him assume an obligation that he likely cannot meet? Should we assist him directly in some other way? Many people, including both signers and cosigners, wish they had followed such good advice.

In our personal economic affairs, the combination of hard work and common sense will serve us well.

Proverbs

Industriousness

Go to the ant, you sluggard;
>consider its ways and be wise!
It has no commander,
>no overseer or ruler,
yet it stores its provisions in summer
>and gathers its food at harvest.

How long will you lie there, you sluggard?
>When will you get up from your sleep?
A little sleep, a little slumber,
>a little folding of the hands to rest—
and poverty will come on you like a bandit
>and scarcity like an armed man.

PROVERBS 6:6-11

Lazy hands make a man poor,
>but diligent hands bring wealth.

He who gathers crops in summer is a wise son,
>but he who sleeps during harvest is a disgraceful
>son.

PROVERBS 10:4-5

As vinegar to the teeth and smoke to the eyes,
  so is a sluggard to those who send him.
                                    PROVERBS 10:26

He who works his land will have abundant food,
  but he who chases fantasies lacks judgment.
                                    PROVERBS 12:11

Diligent hands will rule,
  but laziness ends in slave labor.
                                    PROVERBS 12:24

The lazy man does not roast his game,
  but the diligent man prizes his possessions.
                                    PROVERBS 12:27

The sluggard craves and gets nothing,
  but the desires of the diligent are fully satisfied.
                                    PROVERBS 13:4

Where there are no oxen, the manger is empty,
  but from the strength of an ox comes an abundant
    harvest.
                                    PROVERBS 14:4

All hard work brings a profit,
  but mere talk leads only to poverty.
                                    PROVERBS 14:23

The way of the sluggard is blocked with thorns,
  but the path of the upright is a highway.
                                    PROVERBS 15:19

The laborer's appetite works for him;
  his hunger drives him on.
                                    PROVERBS 16:26

One who is slack in his work
　　is brother to one who destroys.

Proverbs 18:9

Laziness brings on deep sleep,
　　and the shiftless man goes hungry.

Proverbs 19:15

The sluggard buries his hand in the dish;
　　he will not even bring it back to his mouth!

Proverbs 19:24; 26:15

A sluggard does not plow in season;
　　so at harvest time he looks but finds nothing.

Proverbs 20:4

Do not love sleep or you will grow poor;
　　stay awake and you will have food to spare.

Proverbs 20:13

He who loves pleasure will become poor;
　　whoever loves wine and oil will never be rich.

Proverbs 21:17

The sluggard's craving will be the death of him,
　　because his hands refuse to work.
All day long he craves for more,
　　but the righteous give without sparing.

Proverbs 21:25-26

Do you see a man skilled in his work?
　　He will serve before kings;
　　he will not serve before obscure men.

Proverbs 22:29

Finish your outdoor work
  and get your fields ready;
  after that, build your house.

PROVERBS 24:27

I went past the field of the sluggard,
  past the vineyard of the man who lacks judgment;
thorns had come up everywhere,
  the ground was covered with weeds,
  and the stone wall was in ruins.
I applied my heart to what I observed
  and learned a lesson from what I saw:
A little sleep, a little slumber,
  a little folding of the hands to rest—
and poverty will come on you like a bandit
  and scarcity like an armed man.

PROVERBS 24:30-34

As a door turns on its hinges,
  so a sluggard turns on his bed.

PROVERBS 26:14

He who tends a fig tree will eat its fruit,
  and he who looks after his master will be honored.

PROVERBS 27:18

Be sure you know the condition of your flocks,
  give careful attention to your herds;
for riches do not endure forever,
  and a crown is not secure for all generations.
When the hay is removed and new growth appears
  and the grass from the hills is gathered in,
the lambs will provide you with clothing,
  and the goats with the price of a field.
You will have plenty of goats' milk

to feed you and your family
and to nourish your servant girls.

PROVERBS 27:23-27

He who works his land will have abundant food,
but the one who chases fantasies will have his fill
of poverty.

PROVERBS 28:19

Conservation

In the house of the wise are stores of choice food and
oil,
but a foolish man devours all he has.

PROVERBS 21:20

Surety for Another

My son, if you have put up security for your neighbor,
if you have struck hands in pledge for another,
if you have been trapped by what you said,
ensnared by the words of your mouth,
then do this, my son, to free yourself,
since you have fallen into your neighbor's hands:
Go and humble yourself;
press your plea with your neighbor!
Allow no sleep to your eyes,
no slumber to your eyelids.
Free yourself, like a gazelle from the hand of the
hunter,
like a bird from the snare of the fowler.

PROVERBS 6:1-5

He who puts up security for another will surely suffer,
but whoever refuses to strike hands in pledge is
safe.

PROVERBS 11:15

A man lacking in judgment strikes hands in pledge
and puts up security for his neighbor.

PROVERBS 17:18

Take the garment of one who puts up security for a
stranger;
hold it in pledge if he does it for a wayward
woman.

PROVERBS 20:16; 27:13

Do not be a man who strikes hands in pledge
or puts up security for debts;
if you lack the means to pay,
your very bed will be snatched from under you.

PROVERBS 22:26-27

Psalms

AS WE ARE ABOUT TO BE REMINDED IN THE NEXT psalm, truly
righteous people are rewarded for being industrious and
generous. If nothing else, working hard just makes good
sense. What has anyone gained from being lazy? On the
other hand, what happens when we get the idea that all
good things come by working for them? Are we to think
that our spiritual blessings are also the result of work—the
kind of work of which we could boast? And if we do some
good work, do we perhaps feel entitled to God's good
mercies?

In our saner moments, we all know that's not how
God's grace-based economy works. With His usual irony,
God cautions us not to be cosigners for the debts of others,
then turns right around and "cosigns" *our* spiritual
poverty—a debt which we ourselves could never repay!

Better the little that the righteous have
　　than the wealth of many wicked;
for the power of the wicked will be broken,
　　but the Lord upholds the righteous.

The days of the blameless are known to the Lord,
　　and their inheritance will endure forever.
In times of disaster they will not wither;
　　in days of famine they will enjoy plenty.

But the wicked will perish:
　　The Lord's enemies will be like the beauty of the
　　　　fields,
　　they will vanish—vanish like smoke.

The wicked borrow and do not repay,
　　but the righteous give generously;
those the Lord blesses will inherit the land,
　　but those he curses will be cut off.

If the Lord delights in a man's way,
　　he makes his steps firm;
though he stumble, he will not fall,
　　for the Lord upholds him with his hand.

I was young and now I am old,
　　yet I have never seen the righteous forsaken
　　or their children begging bread.
They are always generous and lend freely;
　　their children will be blessed.

Psalm 37:16-26

Abundant Family Relationships

W̲HAT IS THE BEST ADVICE YOUR PARENTS EVER gave you? Did you recognize its value at the time? Did you follow the advice? If not, did you later regret it? Parental advice comes sometimes by way of example and sometimes by expectations. However it is given, a parent's advice is usually uncannily accurate. How did our parents know so much? Who made them so wise?

We usually appreciate our parents more after we become adults or have children than when we are young. Thanking them for what they have done is not always possible or easy. Our lives should reward them for their advice and concern.

Children are a risky investment, and the stakes are high. Some children cruelly turn against their parents and despise them. But parents experience their greatest joy and satisfaction when their children make them proud.

Success obviously bring joy. But failure is more complicated. Do children rebel because they are not given the right instruction? Does an inconsistent example put a cloud on what is taught? Is one child more receptive than another? Are environments away from the home too influential to overcome? Good parents may share in the responsibility for children gone bad. They may have contributed to their own grief. But God clearly demonstrates that each person is ultimately responsible for his own conduct. Parents who have given godly advice, have lived godly lives, and have prayed godly prayers for their children have done all that God has asked.

Realizing this limitation on a parent's duty will not diminish the hurt, but understanding it should lessen the guilt. As God's children, we know we greatly grieve God by our continual acts of rebellion. Yet who would blame God for what we do?

Praise God for good parents and for the lessons they taught us. Praise God when He has adopted us as children of His own!

Proverbs

Parents and Children

Listen, my son, to your father's instruction
    and do not forsake your mother's teaching.
They will be a garland to grace your head
    and a chain to adorn your neck.

Proverbs 1:8-9

A wise son brings joy to his father,
    but a foolish son grief to his mother.

Proverbs 10:1

He who brings trouble on his family will inherit only wind,
    and the fool will be servant to the wise.

Proverbs 11:29

A wise son brings joy to his father,
    but a foolish man despises his mother.

Proverbs 15:20

A wise servant will rule over a disgraceful son,
   and will share the inheritance as one of the
      brothers.

PROVERBS 17:2

Children's children are a crown to the aged,
   and parents are the pride of their children.

PROVERBS 17:6

To have a fool for a son brings grief;
   there is no joy for the father of a fool.

PROVERBS 17:21

A foolish son brings grief to his father
   and bitterness to the one who bore him.

PROVERBS 17:25

He who robs his father and drives out his mother
   is a son who brings shame and disgrace.

PROVERBS 19:26

If a man curses his father or mother,
   his lamp will be snuffed out in pitch darkness.

PROVERBS 20:20

Listen to your father, who gave you life,
   and do not despise your mother when she is old.
Buy the truth and do not sell it;
   get wisdom, discipline and understanding.
The father of a righteous man has great joy;
   he who has a wise son delights in him.
May your father and mother be glad;
   may she who gave you birth rejoice!

PROVERBS 23:22-25

He who robs his father or mother
and says, "It's not wrong"—
he is partner to him who destroys.

Proverbs 28:24

The Elderly

Gray hair is a crown of splendor;
it is attained by a righteous life.

Proverbs 16:31

The glory of young men is their strength,
gray hair the splendor of the old.

Proverbs 20:29

Women and Wives

Like a gold ring in a pig's snout
is a beautiful woman who shows no discretion.

Proverbs 11:22

A wife of noble character is her husband's crown,
but a disgraceful wife is like decay in his bones.

Proverbs 12:4

The wise woman builds her house,
but with her own hands the foolish one tears hers
down.

Proverbs 14:1

He who finds a wife finds what is good
and receives favor from the Lord.

Proverbs 18:22

A foolish son is his father's ruin,
    and a quarrelsome wife is like a constant dripping.

Houses and wealth are inherited from parents,
    but a prudent wife is from the LORD.

PROVERBS 19:13-14

Better to live on a corner of the roof
    than share a house with a quarrelsome wife.

PROVERBS 21:9; 25:24

Better to live in a desert
    than with a quarrelsome and ill-tempered wife.

PROVERBS 21:19

A quarrelsome wife is like
    a constant dripping on a rainy day;
restraining her is like restraining the wind
    or grasping oil with the hand.

PROVERBS 27:15-16

THAT LAST SECTION ABOUT QUARRELSOME WIVES seems more fitting for *Taming of the Shrew* than the "Abundant Family Relationships" that the chapter title promised. In Shakespeare's play, Petruchio has to wean Katherine away from her tempestuous and quarrelsome nature. How he achieves that result is similar to the way in which parents must "tame" the young through instruction, discipline, good humor, and love.

Just as the play has a happy ending, this next brief psalm speaks of a peace of mind that David enjoys when he finally humbles himself in the face of questions too ponderous for him to get his head around. And to what does he compare his state of mind? To a weaned child. To a child who has escaped the self-willed rebellion of "the terrible twos" and has begun to appreciate those first dim rays of an adult perspective. How proud our heavenly Father must be of us when He sees us wisely yielding ourselves to His leading. A felicitous taming of the *shrewd*, perhaps?

My heart is not proud, O Lord,
    my eyes are not haughty;
I do not concern myself with great matters
    or things too wonderful for me.
But I have stilled and quieted my soul;
    like a weaned child with its mother,
    like a weaned child is my soul within me.

O Israel, put your hope in the Lord
    both now and forevermore.

Psalm 131

God's Wonderful Woman

WHO IS THE MOST WONDERFUL WOMAN YOU have known? What is there about her that commands your respect? What character qualities set her apart from all others? Where did she get her strength and dignity? What motivates her service to others?

The writer's praise of a wonderful woman focuses not on her physical beauty but on the beauty of her inner person. The praise is for a woman who works tirelessly for her family. A woman who handles her business affairs prudently and is the pride of her husband. A benevolent and hospitable woman who keeps her eyes on the needs of others. An intelligent woman with good advice to share. A woman who has the respect of her children.

What motivates this wonderful woman? Her husband, yes, and her children as well. But her relationship with God is what guides and sustains her. It is her understanding of Wisdom that makes her so special. In this she is an example to us all.

Proverbs

A Parable of a God Who Provides

A wife of noble character who can find?
She is worth far more than rubies.

Her husband has full confidence in her
    and lacks nothing of value.
She brings him good, not harm,
    all the days of her life.
She selects wool and flax
    and works with eager hands.
She is like the merchant ships,
    bringing her food from afar.
She gets up while it is still dark;
    she provides food for her family
    and portions for her servant girls.
She considers a field and buys it;
    out of her earnings she plants a vineyard.
She sets about her work vigorously;
    her arms are strong for her tasks.
She sees that her trading is profitable,
    and her lamp does not go out at night.
In her hand she holds the distaff
    and grasps the spindle with her fingers.
She opens her arms to the poor
    and extends her hands to the needy.
When it snows, she has no fear for her household;
    for all of them are clothed in scarlet.
She makes coverings for her bed;
    she is clothed in fine linen and purple.
Her husband is respected at the city gate,
    where he takes his seat among the elders of the
        land.
She makes linen garments and sells them,
    and supplies the merchants with sashes.
She is clothed with strength and dignity;
    she can laugh at the days to come.
She speaks with wisdom,
    and faithful instruction is on her tongue.
She watches over the affairs of her household
    and does not eat the bread of idleness.

Her children arise and call her blessed;
    her husband also, and he praises her:
"Many women do noble things,
    but you surpass them all."
Charm is deceptive, and beauty is fleeting;
    but a woman who fears the LORD is to be praised.
Give her the reward she has earned,
    and let her works bring her praise at the city gate.
                              PROVERBS 31:10-31

Psalms

JUST READING ABOUT ALL THE WONDERFUL THINGS this godly, industrious woman accomplishes in a 24-hour period is exhausting! No wonder her husband and children praise her. Indeed, who wouldn't praise her? Would anyone be so cynical as to deny that her value is far above that of rubies? Would anyone at all show disdain for the gracious and loving works of her hands?

If not, then why would anyone be so cynical as to deny the handiwork of God so evident throughout His creation? "God's wonderful woman" of Psalm 31 is but a parable of God Himself and how His divine power never ceases to provide for our every need. When we stop long enough to fully appreciate the mighty works of God's hand, we cannot help but join in with the opening line of this stirring psalm. Who, but a self-exalting fool, would not join in?

Praise the LORD, O my soul.

O LORD my God, you are very great;
    you are clothed with splendor and majesty.
He wraps himself in light as with a garment;

he stretches out the heavens like a tent
and lays the beams of his upper chambers on their
waters.
He makes the clouds his chariot
and rides on the wings of the wind.
He makes winds his messengers,
flames of fire his servants.

He set the earth on its foundations;
it can never be moved.
You covered it with the deep as with a garment;
the waters stood above the mountains.
But at your rebuke the waters fled,
at the sound of your thunder they took to flight;
they flowed over the mountains,
they went down into the valleys,
to the place you assigned for them.
You set a boundary they cannot cross;
never again will they cover the earth.

He makes springs pour water into the ravines;
it flows between the mountains.
They give water to all the beasts of the field;
the wild donkeys quench their thirst.
The birds of the air nest by the waters;
they sing among the branches.
He waters the mountains from his upper chambers;
the earth is satisfied by the fruit of his work.
He makes grass grow for the cattle,
and plants for man to cultivate—
bringing forth food from the earth:
wine that gladdens the heart of man,
oil to make his face shine,
and bread that sustains his heart.
The trees of the LORD are well watered,
the cedars of Lebanon that he planted.

There the birds make their nests;
    the stork has its home in the pine trees.
The high mountains belong to the wild goats;
    the crags are a refuge for the coneys.

The moon marks off the seasons,
    and the sun knows when to go down.
You bring darkness, it becomes night,
    and all the beasts of the forest prowl.
The lions roar for their prey
    and seek their food from God.
The sun rises, and they steal away;
    they return and lie down in their dens.
Then man goes out to his work,
    to his labor until evening.

How many are your works, O LORD!
    In wisdom you made them all;
    the earth is full of your creatures.
There is the sea, vast and spacious,
    teeming with creatures beyond number—
    living things both large and small.
There the ships go to and fro,
    and the leviathan, which you formed to frolic
        there.

These all look to you
    to give them their food at the proper time.
When you give it to them,
    they gather it up;
when you open your hand,
    they are satisfied with good things.
When you hide your face,
    they are terrified;
when you take away their breath,
    they die and return to the dust.

When you send your Spirit,
    they are created,
    and you renew the face of the earth.

May the glory of the LORD endure forever;
    may the LORD rejoice in his works—
he who looks at the earth, and it trembles,
    who touches the mountains, and they smoke.

I will sing to the LORD all my life;
    I will sing praise to my God as long as I live.
May my meditation be pleasing to him,
    as I rejoice in the LORD.
But may sinners vanish from the earth
    and the wicked be no more.

Praise the LORD, O my soul.

Praise the LORD.

PSALM 104

Keeping the Wedding Vows Alive

IF YOU ARE MARRIED, HAVE YOU EVER THOUGHT ABOUT committing adultery? So many people have "affairs" (an innocent-sounding euphemism) these days that they no longer shock us. Movies and television regularly portray guilt-free adultery.

The intriguing question is, Why? Why would someone want to have an affair? For the excitement of illicit pleasure? Because your marriage is boring or your spouse is not a satisfactory lover? Or just greed for what someone else has?

An emotional relationship sometimes leads to temptation. Even good people get tripped up, especially if they are in an unfulfilling marriage. After years of one spouse being at the office all night, the one waiting at home may no longer be waiting. And constant criticism will drive a person straight into more understanding arms.

Whatever the apparent reason, the real reason may have more to do with the allure of adultery. Seduction is successful because it is so terribly seductive. It looks so good, feels so warm, seems so right. But truth in advertising would ruin adultery's commercials. The truth is that adultery is a fraud. It never delivers what it promises. It doesn't make you happy because it loads you down with guilt and fear of discovery. It doesn't satisfy because it lacks a proper relationship to sustain it. It is not fun because too many people get hurt. It doesn't renew a lifeless marriage because the frustration is only enhanced by thinking of what might be.

No wonder Solomon singles out adultery for special warning. After all, his father and mother were two of history's best-known adulterers. What advice does Solomon give to one who might be thinking of having an affair? First, don't even think about it. Second, don't let yourself get anywhere near its temptation. Magnets have no attraction when kept in separate places. Third, think a long time about the consequences. Any one of the inevitable consequences should be enough to persuade you to remain faithful.

The best defense, of course, is to enrich your own marriage. Solomon suggests a renewed effort at recognizing what you have. What brought the two of you together in the first place? It must have been something special. When you lose something special, don't you try to find it?

Proverbs

Adultery

My son, pay attention to my wisdom,
    listen well to my words of insight,
that you may maintain discretion
    and your lips may preserve knowledge.
For the lips of an adulteress drip honey,
    and her speech is smoother than oil;
but in the end she is bitter as gall,
    sharp as a double-edged sword.
Her feet go down to death;
    her steps lead straight to the grave.

She gives no thought to the way of life;
    her paths are crooked, but she knows it not.

Now then, my sons, listen to me;
    do not turn aside from what I say.
Keep to a path far from her,
    do not go near the door of her house,
lest you give your best strength to others
    and your years to one who is cruel,
lest strangers feast on your wealth
    and your toil enrich another man's house.
At the end of your life you will groan,
    when your flesh and body are spent.
You will say, "How I hated discipline!
    How my heart spurned correction!
I would not obey my teachers
    or listen to my instructors.
I have come to the brink of utter ruin
    in the midst of the whole assembly."

Drink water from your own cistern,
    running water from your own well.
Should your springs overflow in the streets,
    your streams of water in the public squares?
Let them be yours alone,
    never to be shared with strangers.
May your fountain be blessed,
    and may you rejoice in the wife of your youth.
A loving doe, a graceful deer—
    may her breasts satisfy you always,
    may you ever be captivated by her love.
Why be captivated, my son, by an adulteress?
    Why embrace the bosom of another man's wife?

For a man's ways are in full view of the LORD,
    and he examines all his paths.

The evil deeds of a wicked man ensnare him;
    the cords of his sin hold him fast.
He will die for lack of discipline,
    led astray by his own great folly.

PROVERBS 5:1-23

My son, keep your father's commands
    and do not forsake your mother's teaching.
Bind them upon your heart forever;
    fasten them around your neck.
When you walk, they will guide you;
    when you sleep, they will watch over you;
    when you awake, they will speak to you.
For these commands are a lamp,
    this teaching is a light,
and the corrections of discipline
    are the way to life,
keeping you from the immoral woman,
    from the smooth tongue of the wayward wife.
Do not lust in your heart after her beauty
    or let her captivate you with her eyes,
for the prostitute reduces you to a loaf of bread,
    and the adulteress preys upon your very life.
Can a man scoop fire into his lap
    without his clothes being burned?
Can a man walk on hot coals
    without his feet being scorched?
So is he who sleeps with another man's wife;
    no one who touches her will go unpunished.

Men do not despise a thief if he steals
    to satisfy his hunger when he is starving.
Yet if he is caught, he must pay sevenfold,
    though it costs him all the wealth of his house.
But a man who commits adultery lacks judgment;
    whoever does so destroys himself.

Blows and disgrace are his lot,
    and his shame will never be wiped away;
for jealousy arouses a husband's fury,
        and he will show no mercy when he takes
            revenge.
He will not accept any compensation;
    he will refuse the bribe, however great it is.

PROVERBS 6:20-35

My son, keep my words
    and store up my commands within you.
Keep my commands and you will live;
    guard my teachings as the apple of your eye.
Bind them on your fingers;
    write them on the tablet of your heart.
Say to wisdom, "You are my sister,"
    and call understanding your kinsman;
they will keep you from the adulteress,
    from the wayward wife with her seductive words.

At the window of my house
    I looked out through the lattice.
I saw among the simple,
    I noticed among the young men,
    a youth who lacked judgment.
He was going down the street near her corner,
    walking along in the direction of her house
at twilight, as the day was fading,
    as the dark of night set in.

Then out came a woman to meet him,
    dressed like a prostitute and with crafty intent.
(She is loud and defiant,
    her feet never stay at home;
now in the street, now in the squares,
    at every corner she lurks.)

She took hold of him and kissed him
    and with a brazen face she said:

"I have fellowship offerings at home;
    today I fulfilled my vows.
So I came out to meet you;
    I looked for you and have found you!
I have covered my bed
    with colored linens from Egypt.
I have perfumed my bed
    with myrrh, aloes and cinnamon.
Come, let's drink deep of love till morning;
    let's enjoy ourselves with love!
My husband is not at home;
    he has gone on a long journey
He took his purse filled with money
    and will not be home till full moon."

With persuasive words she led him astray;
    she seduced him with her smooth talk.
All at once he followed her
    like an ox going to the slaughter,
like a deer stepping into a noose
    till an arrow pierces his liver,
like a bird darting into a snare,
    little knowing it will cost him his life.

Now then, my sons, listen to me;
    pay attention to what I say.
Do not let your heart turn to her ways
    or stray into her paths.
Many are the victims she has brought down;
    her slain are a mighty throng.
Her house is a highway to the grave,
    leading down to the chambers of death.

Proverbs 7:1-27

The mouth of an adulteress is a deep pit;
he who is under the LORD's wrath will fall into it.

PROVERBS 22:14

Prostitution

My son, give me your heart
and let your eyes keep to my ways,
for a prostitute is a deep pit
and a wayward wife is a narrow well.
Like a bandit she lies in wait,
and multiplies the unfaithful among men.

PROVERBS 23:26-28

A man who loves wisdom brings joy to his father,
but a companion of prostitutes squanders his
wealth.

PROVERBS 29:3

OF ALL OF DAVID'S PSALMS, PERHAPS THE MOST soulful and
revealing is the familiar Psalm 51. It is one of only a few
psalms in which the specific setting is revealed. In this
instance, David candidly exposes his deep sense of guilt
and remorse over his notorious sin with Bathsheba.
Whereas various proverbs often paint a picture of the
seducing wife drawing an unsuspecting man into her bed,
everyone knows that David himself lusted after Bathsheba
and did whatever he needed to have her.

As David finally comes to his senses at the prompting
of Nathan the prophet, he is so stricken with guilt that,
employing anguished hyperbole, he laments that surely

he must have been sinful from the moment his mother first conceived him. Of course, it was sin in a different womb that had brought him such devastation of spirit. But even in this tortured exaggeration, David speaks a profound truth. His sin didn't begin in Bathsheba's arms. It began at the moment of conception—at the moment he took that first forbidden look at her beauty and conceived to have her, regardless of the consequences.

In this poignant plea for greater purity, of course, David is not alone. For all that we, too, have conceived in our hearts, Lord, have mercy!

Have mercy on me, O God,
according to your unfailing love;
according to your great compassion
blot out my transgressions.
Wash away all my iniquity
and cleanse me from my sin.

For I know my transgressions,
and my sin is always before me.
Against you, you only, have I sinned
and done what is evil in your sight,
so that you are proved right when you speak
and justified when you judge.
Surely I was sinful at birth,
sinful from the time my mother conceived me.
Surely you desire truth in the inner parts;
you teach me wisdom in the inmost place.

Cleanse me with hyssop, and I will be clean;
wash me, and I will be whiter than snow.
Let me hear joy and gladness;
let the bones you have crushed rejoice.
Hide your face from my sins
and blot out all my iniquity.

Create in me a pure heart, O God,
     and renew a steadfast spirit within me.
Do not cast me from your presence
     or take your Holy Spirit from me.
Restore to me the joy of your salvation
     and grant me a willing spirit, to sustain me.

Then I will teach transgressors your ways,
     and sinners will turn back to you.
Save me from bloodguilt, O God,
     the God who saves me,
     and my tongue will sing of your righteousness.
O Lord, open my lips,
     and my mouth will declare your praise.
You do not delight in sacrifice, or I would bring it;
     you do not take pleasure in burnt offerings.
The sacrifices of God are a broken spirit;
     a broken and contrite heart,
     O God, you will not despise.

In your good pleasure make Zion prosper;
     build up the walls of Jerusalem.
Then there will be righteous sacrifices,
     whole burnt offerings to delight you;
     then bulls will be offered on your altar.

PSALM 51

The Treasures of Friendship

WHO IS YOUR BEST FRIEND? WHY ARE THE TWO of you so close? Have you shared difficult times together? Do you have any secrets you couldn't tell your friend? Is advice from your friend easier to accept than advice from other people? Those are the very things that make best friends. This is why Solomon says that a good friend can sometimes be closer than a relative. Having an extended family of good friends is a tremendous blessing. In times of trouble, they are a life-support system. In good times, they share the joy.

Are you without a best friend? Do you sometimes feel as if you have no friends at all? One Person has shared in every bad experience you have ever had. You can tell Him anything—even that you don't like Him sometimes or that you don't always understand His actions or His demands on you. He offers the best advice, and He is always near. Of course, this Friend is God.

"But it is not the same," you say. "I need someone to share a cup of coffee with, or to give me a hug when I'm feeling down." Sure you do. We all do. And God's hugs are not quite the same. But He has also provided hugs and companionship through others around us—perhaps someone next door or down the street who is also lonely. Are we supposed to wait until they find us? They are waiting for someone to knock on their door. We should be the ones to do that.

Proverbs

Companions

A righteous man is cautious in friendship,
> but the way of the wicked leads them astray.
>> PROVERBS 12:26

He who walks with the wise grows wise,
> but a companion of fools suffers harm.
>> PROVERBS 13:20

Stay away from a foolish man,
> for you will not find knowledge on his lips.
>> PROVERBS 14:7

A friend loves at all times,
> and a brother is born for adversity.
>> PROVERBS 17:17

A man of many companions may come to ruin,
> but there is a friend who sticks closer than a
>> brother.
>>> PROVERBS 18:24

Do not envy wicked men,
> do not desire their company;
for their hearts plot violence,
> and their lips talk about making trouble.
>> PROVERBS 24:1-2

Like a bird that strays from its nest
>   is a man who strays from his home.

Perfume and incense bring joy to the heart,
>   and the pleasantness of one's friend springs from
>   his earnest counsel.

Do not forsake your friend and the friend of your
>   father,
>   and do not go to your brother's house when
>   disaster strikes you—
>   better a neighbor nearby than a brother far away.
>   PROVERBS 27:8-10

The accomplice of a thief is his own enemy;
>   he is put under oath and dare not testify.
>   PROVERBS 29:24

Psalms

ALMOST NOTHING IS AS DEBILITATING AS PROLONGED, pervasive loneliness. Oddly enough, that kind of loneliness can be felt deeply even in the midst of a crowd, a marriage, or a family. Yet, typically, extreme loneliness haunts those who are literally alone, whether for lack, or loss, of a marriage partner, or because of advancing age or ill health. The question of marriage aside, being alone simply isn't good for us. We were created as social beings and intended for companionship. Set first in families to meet that need, we are then blessed with a wider circle of friends and companions to help fill up our senses and hold on to the mast together in the midst of life's storms.

But when even our closest companions are no longer near, where can we turn to chase away the haunting loneliness that envelops us? If the answer is obvious, it is equally profound. The very notion that our Maker is also our closest personal companion—so vastly distant yet so very near—is truly beyond comprehension. Yet in the forlorn darkness of a lonely night, or in the turbulence and fear of life's many storms, the only hand you may feel just might be divine.

Listen to my prayer, O God,
do not ignore my plea;
hear me and answer me.
My thoughts trouble me and I am distraught
at the voice of the enemy,
at the stares of the wicked;
for they bring down suffering upon me
and revile me in their anger.

My heart is in anguish within me;
the terrors of death assail me.
Fear and trembling have beset me;
horror has overwhelmed me.
I said, "Oh, that I had the wings of a dove!
I would fly away and be at rest—
I would flee far away
and stay in the desert;   *Selah*
I would hurry to my place of shelter,
far from the tempest and storm."

Confuse the wicked, O Lord, confound their speech,
for I see violence and strife in the city.
Day and night they prowl about on its walls;
malice and abuse are within it.
Destructive forces are at work in the city;
threats and lies never leave its streets.

THE TREASURES OF FRIENDSHIP

If an enemy were insulting me,
      I could endure it;
if a foe were raising himself against me,
      I could hide from him.
But it is you, a man like myself,
      my companion, my close friend,
with whom I once enjoyed sweet fellowship
      as we walked with the throng at the house of God.

Let death take my enemies by surprise;
      let them go down alive to the grave,
      for evil finds lodging among them.

But I call to God,
      and the LORD saves me.
Evening, morning and noon
      I cry out in distress,
      and he hears my voice.
He ransoms me unharmed
      from the battle waged against me,
      even though many oppose me.
God, who is enthroned forever,
      will hear them and afflict them—   *Selah*
men who never change their ways
      and have no fear of God.

My companion attacks his friends;
      he violates his covenant.
His speech is smooth as butter,
      yet war is in his heart;
his words are more soothing than oil,
      yet they are drawn swords.

Cast your cares on the LORD
      and he will sustain you;
      he will never let the righteous fall.

But you, O God, will bring down the wicked
    into the pit of corruption;
bloodthirsty and deceitful men
    will not live out half their days.

But as for me, I trust in you.

PSALM 55

Toward Godly Leadership

SOLOMON, A GREAT POLITICAL LEADER LIKE HIS FATHER, King David, had much to say about those who rule. He insisted that a ruler's great power demands a heightened sense of justice and an unlimited concern for the poor. He suggested that the wise ruler will concentrate on bringing order to his nation and provide strong moral leadership that is free from bribes, dishonesty, and arrogance. Above all, the king must remember that he rules by God's favor. He must never forget that as an instrument of God he is subject to exceptional accountability and that his tenure as a leader is always subject to God's approval.

In Proverbs we also find advice from King Lemuel's mother, who was fearful that her son's high position of leadership would make him forget who he was. The wisdom she gives Lemuel is appropriate for us all. Few of us will ever be in positions of political leadership, but many of us are in various other positions of leadership, whether in the family, the church, our jobs, or social organizations. What can we learn from the leadership wisdom found within the following proverbs?

Kings and Rulers

A large population is a king's glory,
    but without subjects a prince is ruined.

PROVERBS 14:28

A king delights in a wise servant,
    but a shameful servant incurs his wrath.

PROVERBS 14:35

The lips of a king speak as an oracle,
    and his mouth should not betray justice.

PROVERBS 16:10

Kings detest wrongdoing,
    for a throne is established through righteousness.

Kings take pleasure in honest lips;
    they value a man who speaks the truth.

A king's wrath is a messenger of death,
    but a wise man will appease it.

When a king's face brightens, it means life;
    his favor is like a rain cloud in spring.

PROVERBS 16:12-15

Arrogant lips are unsuited to a fool—
    how much worse lying lips to a ruler!

PROVERBS 17:7

An evil man is bent only on rebellion;
    a merciless official will be sent against him.

PROVERBS 17:11

A king's rage is like the roar of a lion,
    but his favor is like dew on the grass.

PROVERBS 19:12

A king's wrath is like the roar of a lion;
    he who angers him forfeits his life.

PROVERBS 20:2

When a king sits on his throne to judge,
    he winnows out all evil with his eyes.

PROVERBS 20:8

A wise king winnows out the wicked;
    he drives the threshing wheel over them.

PROVERBS 20:26

Love and faithfulness keep a king safe;
    through love his throne is made secure.

PROVERBS 20:28

The king's heart is in the hand of the LORD,
    he directs it like a watercourse wherever he
        pleases.

PROVERBS 21:1

He who loves a pure heart and whose speech is
        gracious
    will have the king for his friend.

PROVERBS 22:11

When you sit to dine with a ruler,
    note well what is before you,
and put a knife to your throat
    if you are given to gluttony.
Do not crave his delicacies,
    for the food is deceptive.

PROVERBS 23:1-3

Fear the LORD and the king, my son,
    and do not join with the rebellious,
for those two will send sudden destruction upon them,
    and who knows what calamities they can bring?
                PROVERBS 24:21-22

It is the glory of God to conceal a matter;
    to search out a matter is the glory of kings.

As the heavens are high and the earth is deep,
    so the hearts of kings are unsearchable.

Remove the dross from the silver,
    and out comes material for the silversmith;
remove the wicked from the king's presence,
    and his throne will be established through
        righteousness.

Do not exalt yourself in the king's presence,
    and do not claim a place among great men;
it is better for him to say to you, "Come up here,"
    than for him to humiliate you before a nobleman.
                PROVERBS 25:2-7

When a country is rebellious, it has many rulers,
    but a man of understanding and knowledge
        maintains order.

A ruler who oppresses the poor
    is like a driving rain that leaves no crops.
                PROVERBS 28:2-3

Like a roaring lion or a charging bear
    is a wicked man ruling over a helpless people.

A tyrannical ruler lacks judgment,
    but he who hates ill-gotten gain will
        enjoy a long life.

PROVERBS 28:15-16

By justice a king gives a country stability,
    but one who is greedy for bribes tears it down.

PROVERBS 29:4

If a ruler listens to lies,
    all his officials become wicked.

PROVERBS 29:12

If a king judges the poor with fairness,
    his throne will always be secure.

PROVERBS 29:14

Messengers

A wicked messenger falls into trouble,
    but a trustworthy envoy brings healing.

PROVERBS 13:17

Like the coolness of snow at harvest time
    is a trustworthy messenger to those who send him;
    he refreshes the spirit of his masters.

PROVERBS 25:13

A Mother's Advice to a King

The sayings of King Lemuel—an oracle his mother
    taught him:
  "O my son, O son of my womb,
    O son of my vows,
  do not spend your strength on women,
    your vigor on those who ruin kings.

"It is not for kings, O Lemuel—
    not for kings to drink wine,
    not for rulers to crave beer,
lest they drink and forget what the law decrees,
    and deprive all the oppressed of their rights.
Give beer to those who are perishing,
    wine to those who are in anguish;
let them drink and forget their poverty
    and remember their misery no more.

"Speak up for those who cannot speak for themselves,
    for the rights of all who are destitute.
Speak up and judge fairly;
    defend the rights of the poor and needy."

PROVERBS 31:1-9

Psalms

ONE WOULD BE HARD-PRESSED TO FIND A KING who is willing to bow down and do obeisance before another king, but that is exactly what we're about to see when David comes into the presence of God with praise and thanksgiving. Mighty king though he is, David knows that the God of heaven is the one and only King of kings and Ruler over potentates. And so he calls on all kings everywhere to join him in praise of the Mighty One whose words take precedence even over sovereign decrees and kingly proclamations.

Though presidents and prime ministers swear faithfulness to their office with a traditional "so help me God," and kings and queens may even be anointed with oil during an overtly religious coronation, they can only hope to imitate the One by whose sovereign power they themselves rule. That's a high standard for them to follow, but would to God that they at least tried! Then again, what about us? If we claim God as our sovereign Lord, how often do we come into His presence on bended knee and with praise on our lips?

I will praise you, O LORD, with all my heart;
    before the "gods" I will sing your praise.
I will bow down toward your holy temple
    and will praise your name
    for your love and your faithfulness,
for you have exalted above all things
    your name and your word.
When I called, you answered me;
    you made me bold and stouthearted.

May all the kings of the earth praise you, O LORD,
    when they hear the words of your mouth.
May they sing of the ways of the LORD,
    for the glory of the LORD is great.

Though the LORD is on high, he looks upon the lowly,
    but the proud he knows from afar.
Though I walk in the midst of trouble,
    you preserve my life;
you stretch out your hand against the anger of my foes,
    with your right hand you save me.
The LORD will fulfill [his purpose] for me;
    your love, O LORD, endures forever—
    do not abandon the works of your hands.

PSALM 138

God's Complete Care

GOD CARES ABOUT *EVERYTHING* IN OUR LIVES. If He knows each hair on our head, surely He knows when we lock ourselves out of our car. If He is concerned about the tiny insect, does He not care when dinner is burned or sleepy children get fussy? Is anything too trivial for God's attention?

Through the wisdom of Solomon we learn that God cares when He sees us take unnecessary chances. He is concerned with our good reputations and how easily and irrevocably we can lose them. He knows when we are fearful, and He gives us courage and confidence. He knows the value of hope and surprises us with fulfilled dreams to keep our hopes alive. He laughs when we laugh and cries when we cry. He brings us good news to cheer up depressing days and refreshment for our spiritual lives. And to keep us young and active, God gives us childlike curiosity. What a wise and wonderful God we worship!

If you get the idea that this is a "miscellaneous" chapter, you're right. None of the topics included in this section fit very neatly anywhere else. Interestingly enough, sometimes people are that way—not quite fitting in anywhere. We often refer to them as being...well, a bit odd. Have you ever felt a little odd, or peculiar, or out of place? Maybe others have made you feel that way, or perhaps you simply realize how out of step you are with those around you.

Whatever the reason, here's to all the "miscellaneous" people in the world, especially those who believe in Christ. We certainly wouldn't call Jesus of Nazareth "odd" or "strange," but He clearly didn't fit into any neat category. So take hope if you are following in His footsteps. Being called "peculiar people" because we seek to emulate the One who was in a category all His own is without question the most treasured reputation we could ever have.

Caution

The highway of the upright avoids evil;
    he who guards his way guards his life.

            Proverbs 16:17

A prudent man sees danger and takes refuge,
    but the simple keep going and suffer for it.

            Proverbs 22:3; 27:12

In the paths of the wicked lie thorns and snares,
    but he who guards his soul stays far from them.

            Proverbs 22:5

Reputation

A good name is more desirable than great riches;
    to be esteemed is better than silver or gold.

            Proverbs 22:1

If you argue your case with a neighbor,
    do not betray another man's confidence,

or he who hears it may shame you
and you will never lose your bad reputation.
PROVERBS 25:9-10

Courage

Have no fear of sudden disaster
or of the ruin that overtakes the wicked,
for the LORD will be your confidence
and will keep your foot from being snared.
PROVERBS 3:25-26

When calamity comes, the wicked are brought down,
but even in death the righteous have a refuge.
PROVERBS 14:32

The sluggard says, "There is a lion outside!"
or, "I will be murdered in the streets!"
PROVERBS 22:13

If you falter in times of trouble,
how small is your strength!
PROVERBS 24:10

The sluggard says, "There is a lion in the road,
a fierce lion roaming the streets!"
PROVERBS 26:13

The wicked man flees though no one pursues,
but the righteous are as bold as a lion.
PROVERBS 28:1

Hope

Hope deferred makes the heart sick,
but a longing fulfilled is a tree of life.
PROVERBS 13:12

A longing fulfilled is sweet to the soul,
 but fools detest turning from evil.

Proverbs 13:19

Do not let your heart envy sinners,
 but always be zealous for the fear of the Lord.
There is surely a future hope for you,
 and your hope will not be cut off.

Proverbs 23:17-18

Joy and Grief

Each heart knows its own bitterness,
 and no one else can share its joy.

Proverbs 14:10

Even in laughter the heart may ache,
 and joy may end in grief.

Proverbs 14:13

A happy heart makes the face cheerful,
 but heartache crushes the spirit.

Proverbs 15:13

A cheerful heart is good medicine,
 but a crushed spirit dries up the bones.

Proverbs 17:22

A man's spirit sustains him in sickness,
 but a crushed spirit who can bear?

Proverbs 18:14

Like one who takes away a garment on a cold day,
 or like vinegar poured on soda,
  is one who sings songs to a heavy heart.

Proverbs 25:20

Be wise, my son, and bring joy to my heart;
> then I can answer anyone who treats me with
> > contempt.

PROVERBS 27:11

An evil man is snared by his own sin,
> but a righteous one can sing and be glad.

PROVERBS 29:6

Good News

A cheerful look brings joy to the heart,
> and good news gives health to the bones.

PROVERBS 15:30

Like cold water to a weary soul
> is good news from a distant land.

PROVERBS 25:25

Curiosity

Death and Destruction are never satisfied,
> and neither are the eyes of man.

PROVERBS 27:20

Psalms

IN AN AGE OF BIG BROTHER, WHEN CAMERAS AND computers can record our every move, we can find ourselves seeking more and more privacy. Who among us wants to feel that everything we do is subject to someone else's scrutiny? Yet even if David had lived in an era of electronic snooping devices, one gets the feeling that he would not be all that concerned about his privacy—at least not hiding the innermost thoughts of his heart from God. In fact, he invited God to search his heart.

Of course, sometimes we do want to hide. If the subject is lust or hatred within our hearts, we'd just as soon God was not able to see any of that. But if we want God to celebrate our inexpressible joy and sympathize with our unspoken grief, or to give us hope when all hope is gone, or simply to share our good news, then we have to allow Him inside. Besides He already knows us inside out—past, present, and future. So why not trust that, whatever He sees, He puts in the right perspective? Under normal circumstances, hardly anyone likes a know-it-all. But what a different story when Someone really does know it all...and truly cares.

O Lord, you have searched me
    and you know me.
You know when I sit and when I rise;
    you perceive my thoughts from afar.
You discern my going out and my lying down;
    you are familiar with all my ways.
Before a word is on my tongue
    you know it completely, O Lord.

You hem me in—behind and before;
    you have laid your hand upon me.
Such knowledge is too wonderful for me,
    too lofty for me to attain.

Where can I go from your Spirit?
    Where can I flee from your presence?
If I go up to the heavens, you are there;
    if I make my bed in the depths, you are there.
If I rise on the wings of the dawn,
    if I settle on the far side of the sea,

even there your hand will guide me,
    your right hand will hold me fast.

If I say, "Surely the darkness will hide me
    and the light become night around me,"
even the darkness will not be dark to you;
    the night will shine like the day,
    for darkness is as light to you.

For you created my inmost being;
    you knit me together in my mother's womb.
I praise you because I am fearfully and wonderfully
            made;
    your works are wonderful,
    I know that full well.
My frame was not hidden from you
    when I was made in the secret place.
When I was woven together in the depths of the earth,
    your eyes saw my unformed body.
All the days ordained for me
    were written in your book
    before one of them came to be.

How precious to me are your thoughts, O God!
    How vast is the sum of them!
Were I to count them,
    they would outnumber the grains of sand.
When I awake,
    I am still with you.

If only you would slay the wicked, O God!
    Away from me, you bloodthirsty men!
They speak of you with evil intent;
    your adversaries misuse your name.
Do I not hate those who hate you, O LORD,
    and abhor those who rise up against you?

I have nothing but hatred for them;
>   I count them my enemies.

Search me, O God, and know my heart;
>   test me and know my anxious thoughts.
See if there is any offensive way in me,
>   and lead me in the way everlasting.

Psalm 139

A Comforting Life Perspective

HAVE YOU EVER GONE THROUGH SUCH PHYSICAL suffering that you felt abandoned by God? If someone you have loved and depended on has died, have you wondered how God could let it happen? Have you been troubled by how a righteous God can allow evil to exist in the world? Do you sometimes wonder if this life makes any sense at all?

If you have had any of those feelings or ever asked any of those questions, you are in good company. Job and the people in Babylonian captivity shared your doubts. Christian martyrs, victims of the Inquisition, Jews in concentration camps, and millions of political refugees over the centuries have also questioned their suffering and pain. The hospitals, jails, and mental institutions are filled with troubled souls. Few of us, if any, have never questioned life and God's purpose behind it.

With no easy answers, much has to be taken on faith, discouraging as that sometimes can be. But the wisdom of Agur, who experienced difficult struggles himself, reveals some comfort in perspective and humility. When he looked at the universe around him, Agur found it too marvelous to explain. He knew only that God's intelligent creative power is so much greater than our own that we are in no position to fully understand it. If God tells us what to be and how to live, that is the course we should follow. Living any other way would be terribly foolish.

Agur reminds us that God is in control of the universe and that, despite any flaws we think we detect, the universe functions perfectly. We are a part of God's creation, so—despite the questions that may rise—life for us is as it should be. All is well with the world. The answers to our questions will someday bring us knowing smiles.

Entrusting to God Life's Many Mysteries

The sayings of Agur son of Jakeh—an oracle:

This man declared to Ithiel,
to Ithiel and to Ucal:

"I am the most ignorant of men;
I do not have a man's understanding.
I have not learned wisdom,
nor have I knowledge of the Holy One.
Who has gone up to heaven and come down?
Who has gathered up the wind in the hollow of
his hands?
Who has wrapped up the waters in his cloak?
Who has established all the ends of the earth?
What is his name, and the name of his son?
Tell me if you know!

"Every word of God is flawless;
he is a shield to those who take refuge in him.
Do not add to his words,
or he will rebuke you and prove you a liar.

"Two things I ask of you, O LORD;
     do not refuse me before I die:
Keep falsehood and lies far from me;
     give me neither poverty nor riches,
     but give me only my daily bread.
Otherwise, I may have too much and disown you
     and say, 'Who is the LORD?'
Or I may become poor and steal,
     and so dishonor the name of my God.

"Do not slander a servant to his master,
     or he will curse you, and you will pay for it.

"There are those who curse their fathers
     and do not bless their mothers;
those who are pure in their own eyes
     and yet are not cleansed of their filth;
those whose eyes are ever so haughty,
     whose glances are so disdainful;
those whose teeth are swords
     and whose jaws are set with knives
to devour the poor from the earth,
     the needy from among mankind.

"The leech has two daughters.
     'Give! Give!' they cry.

"There are three things that are never satisfied,
     four that never say, 'Enough!':
the grave, the barren womb,
     land, which is never satisfied with water,
     and fire, which never says, 'Enough!'

"The eye that mocks a father,
     that scorns obedience to a mother,

will be pecked out by the ravens of the valley,
    will be eaten by the vultures.

"There are three things that are too amazing for me,
    four that I do not understand;
the way of an eagle in the sky,
    the way of a snake on a rock,
the way of a ship on the high seas,
    and the way of a man with a maiden.

"This is the way of an adulteress:
    She eats and wipes her mouth
    and says, 'I've done nothing wrong.'

"Under three things the earth trembles,
    under four it cannot bear up:
a servant who becomes king,
    a fool who is full of food,
an unloved woman who is married,
    and a maidservant who displaces her mistress.

"Four things on earth are small,
    yet they are extremely wise:
Ants are creatures of little strength,
    yet they store up their food in the summer;
coneys are creatures of little power,
    yet they make their home in the crags;
locusts have no king,
    yet they advance together in ranks;
a lizard can be caught with the hand,
    yet it is found in kings' palaces.

"There are three things that are stately in their stride,
    four that move with stately bearing:
a lion, mighty among beasts,
    who retreats before nothing;

a strutting rooster, a he-goat,
and a king with his army around him.

"If you have played the fool and exalted yourself,
or if you have planned evil,
clap your hand over your mouth!
For as churning the milk produces butter,
and as twisting the nose produces blood,
so stirring up anger produces strife."

PROVERBS 30

Psalms

DID YOU NOTICE A CURIOUS AMBIVALENCE IN AGUR'S claim of unsurpassed ignorance? He might never know many things, but still, he does know much. He knows about leeches and adulteresses and outbursts of anger that stir up conflict. But he is amazed and dumbfounded by life's many mysteries: how eagles fly and snakes slither, how ships can sail through the sea, or even what's so magical (or perhaps so frustrating) between a man and a woman. However, of one thing Agur is fairly sure: No one else has cracked the great mysteries of life either. They are all heaven's secrets, hidden by a masterful Creator who shows us something of His power and intelligence—but ever so little.

In the following psalm—uniquely attributed to Moses— the psalmist reaches out to the Creator of heaven and earth to ask the questions we all want to know about life. Questions, for instance, about death and judgment, about suffering and sin. For all that we don't know, we do know that those are some of the crucial questions that frame our lives and give meaning to our brief existence. Even if we can't know everything about life's great issues, at least we can take comfort in knowing that we have been told all that we truly need to know, and beyond that, God will take care of the rest.

Lord, you have been our dwelling place
    throughout all generations.
Before the mountains were born
    or you brought forth the earth and the world,
    from everlasting to everlasting you are God.

You turn men back to dust,
    saying, "Return to dust, O sons of men."
For a thousand years in your sight
    are like a day that has just gone by,
    or like a watch in the night.
You sweep men away in the sleep of death;
    they are like the new grass of the morning—
though in the morning it springs up new,
    by evening it is dry and withered.

We are consumed by your anger
    and terrified by your indignation.
You have set our iniquities before you,
    our secret sins in the light of your presence.
All our days pass away under your wrath;
    we finish our years with a moan.
The length of our days is seventy years—
    or eighty, if we have the strength;
yet their span is but trouble and sorrow,
    for they quickly pass, and we fly away.

Who knows the power of your anger?
    For your wrath is as great as the fear that is due
        you.

Teach us to number our days aright,
    that we may gain a heart of wisdom.

Relent, O LORD! How long will it be?
    Have compassion on your servants.
Satisfy us in the morning with your unfailing love,
    that we may sing for joy and be glad all our days.
Make us glad for as many days as you have afflicted
        us,
    for as many years as we have seen trouble.
May your deeds be shown to your servants,
    your splendor to their children.

May the favor of the Lord our God rest upon us;
    establish the work of our hands for us—
    yes, establish the work of our hands.

PSALM 90

Index of Psalms and Proverbs

Books You Can Believe In®
HARVEST HOUSE PUBLISHERS

Other Books
by F. LaGard Smith

The Daily Bible®
Featuring the NIV text in a chronological/historical arrangement, this Bible lets you experience history while daily commentary helps you understand God's love and provision.

30 Days with Jesus
In this life-changing Bible study, Smith integrates the four gospels into one chronological narrative to highlight the character and attributes of Jesus. Introduction sections give you an indepth look into the on-earth ministry of Christ.

Meeting God in Quiet Places
In these inspiring parables drawn from his daily walks through the magnificent Cotswolds, LaGard shares life-renewing insights to guide you to the very heart of God. Illustrations refresh the eye and soul.

30 Days through the Bible
In this Bible study, LaGard invites you on a unique 30-day walk through the Bible. Easy-to-read key passages, biblical insights, and devotions explore God's plan, His message, and Scripture's relevance for daily living.